DK GARDEN GUIDES

SHRUBS & CLIMBERS

RICHARD ROSENFELD

**LONDON, NEW YORK,
MUNICH, MELBOURNE, DELHI**

Series Editor Zia Allaway
Series Art Editor Alison Donovan
Managing Editor Anna Kruger
Managing Art Editor Lee Griffiths
Consultant Louise Abbott
DTP Designer Louise Waller
Media Resources Richard Dabb, Lucy Claxton
Picture Research Bridget Tily
Production Controller Mandy Inness
US Editor Christine Heilman
US Senior Editor Jill Hamilton
US Editorial Assistant John Searcy

Produced on behalf of Dorling Kindersley by
HILTON/SADLER
Editorial director: Jonathan Hilton
Design director: Peggy Sadler

Introduction Text Zia Allaway

First American Edition, 2003

Published in the United States by
DK Publishing, Inc.
375 Hudson Street
New York, New York 10014

03 04 05 10 9 8 7 6 5 4 3 2

A Cataloging-in-Publication record for this book
is available from the Library of Congress.

ISBN 0-7894-9345-4

Color reproduction by Colourscan, Singapore
Printed and bound in Italy by Printer Trento

discover more at
www.dk.com

Gardening with shrubs and climbers

For YEAR-ROUND INTEREST in the garden, you can't beat shrubs and climbers. These essential plants provide permanent structure and add height, while also offering flowers, foliage, and fragrance into the bargain. A carefully considered selection will ensure a continuous performance month after month, with catkins and blossoms in spring, flowers throughout the summer, berries and bright foliage in autumn, and a finale in winter of colorful bark, frosted stems, and vivid evergreens.

Whether creating a new border or planning a whole garden, it's best to plant your shrubs and climbers before flowering perennials and annuals, which can be used to fill in the gaps. Choose plants carefully, and make sure they match the site, soil, and space available in your garden. Look carefully at the heights and spreads of your selection, and don't be fooled by the size of plants for sale at garden centers and nurseries, since these are often immature and will grow quickly once planted.

Take note, too, of the seasons in which the plants flower or fruit, so that you can enjoy an evolving display. Foliage is another important consideration, because it has the most enduring effect.

◀ **Small fragrant shrubs,** such as oregano, can be squeezed into paving cracks and small pots.

▶ **Bold, variegated foliage** offers color over a long period, unlike transient flowers.

Using shrubs and climbers

Shrubs and climbers have many uses in gardens large and small, and even a tiny balcony or windowbox will provide space for a small shrub or two. These beautiful plants can either take center stage or form a backdrop for colorful perennials and annuals. They can also help to evoke an atmosphere or create a garden style.

Easy-care shrub borders set against pale gravel are perfect for a low-maintenance garden.

A spiky yucca, for example, will immediately set the scene for an exotic theme, while lavender-edged paths and bay trees will help to define a Mediterranean-style garden.

If you want a low-maintenance garden, make use of easy-care shrubs. Once established, they will swamp

Frosted stems create a magical winter wonderland.

weeds in summer, and many require just light pruning every year or two. Combine plants with different colors and textures in raised beds on a patio or in borders set into gravel to create a long-lasting tapestry effect that will require very little time to care for.

Hedges and edges

Shrubs suitable for hedging, such as laurel (*Prunus laurocerasus*), create natural boundaries around a garden, while a thorny hedge of

Roses and clematis are a match made in heaven, combining colorful flowers with sweet fragrance.

pyracantha has the added benefit of deterring intruders. More compact plants, such as boxwood (*Buxus*) or lavender, also make excellent edging for paths and walkways.

Climbing high

People with small gardens are often afraid to use tall plants, worrying that they will cast too much shade and take up valuable space. If this is a concern for you, consider climbers, which add an important vertical dimension to a garden without taking up too much room, and can be used like wallpaper to decorate fences, walls, sheds, and eyesores. Alternatively, allow them to clamber up trees or through large shrubs.

Pots and patios

Containers planted with shrubs provide an architectural framework for patio displays, and work particularly well as a backdrop to potted flowers. Even big shrubs, such as viburnums, can survive happily in large containers when fed and watered regularly, while small shrubs are useful in windowboxes and baskets, where they make perfect companions for seasonal bedding. Pots filled with acidic soil mix also allow you to grow azaleas and other acid-loving plants in a garden with alkaline soil.

Clothe trellises and arches with leafy climbers to frame a vista punctuated by an urn or sculpture.

Some climbers also do well in large containers. Try the scented star jasmine in a pot close to the back door for a spray of sweet perfume as you step outside. The tender plant can then be easily moved indoors for the winter.

Pots of small hebes offer year-round foliage interest and can be used to set off more seasonal containers.

Choosing shrubs and climbers

WHETHER YOU BUY your shrubs and climbers from a garden center, nursery, or other retail store, take care to select healthy plants that will get off to a good start when planted.

Check the care label to ensure that they are suitable for the site and soil in your garden, since they will soon show signs of stress and may die if grown in the wrong conditions.

Well-balanced, even topgrowth

Well-developed, even framework of stems

Healthy, vigorous foliage, free from damage and disease

Moist soil, free from weed growth

Choosing a healthy plant

When buying plants, reject any that are wilted or have discolored leaves. Make sure no roots are growing out of the bottom of the pot, and tip the plant out to check for a well-developed, healthy root system.

Well-established root system with white root tips. The roots shouldn't be wrapped tightly around the edge

Planting a shrub

Potgrown shrubs can be planted at any time of the year, but ensure that the ground is neither waterlogged nor frozen. Most plants like moist but free-draining soil, but if yours is heavy clay that's prone to waterlogging, increase the drainage by digging in horticultural sand—a wheelbarrowful per 10 sq ft (1 sq m) should do the trick. Free-draining soil can be improved by incorporating well-rotted compost. Water your shrub about an hour before you begin planting.

1 Digging the hole
After improving the soil (see above), choose a dry day to plant your shrub. You will need to dig a hole about twice the width and a little deeper than the root ball.

2 Adding organic matter
Mix the removed soil with organic matter and fork over the base and sides of the hole to loosen the earth. Water the hole and allow the moisture to drain away.

3 Checking the correct depth
Gently ease the shrub out of its container and position it in the hole. Use a stake to check that the plant is at the same depth as it was in its original pot.

4 Finishing off
Backfill around the shrub with the mixed soil and organic matter, firming gently with your heel or hands as you go. Apply a mulch, such as cocoa shells, over the soil.

Planting a climber against a wall

Choosing the right site and soil is as important for climbers as it is for shrubs, but you must also ensure that the plant has adequate support. Check the climber's maximum height for an idea of the size and type of support it requires.

Climbers that cling with tendrils will also need wires or other plants to twine around. When planting, remember that the soil in front of a wall or fence is very dry, and climbers should be placed at least 18in (45cm) away from them.

1 Preparing the site

Prepare the soil as for a shrub, and then dig a hole, 18in (45cm) from the wall, twice as wide as and deeper than the root ball. Add well-rotted compost to the hole.

2 Aligning the climber

Water the climber an hour before planting. Then water the hole, let it drain, and place the plant at a 45° angle. Use a stake to make sure the plant is at the right depth.

3 Tying up

Fill in as you would a shrub, then select four or five strong shoots, and tie in each one to a stake. Attach the stakes to the lowest horizontal wires on the wall.

4 Finishing off

Cut back any weak, damaged, or wayward shoots, and then cover the surrounding soil with a deep mulch, keeping clear the area immediately around the stems.

Caring for shrubs and climbers

FOR THE BEST RESULTS, shrubs and climbers need a little looking after. A suitable site and soil are of primary importance, but watering, feeding, and pruning are also crucial. Water young plants thoroughly when the topsoil feels dry, rather than watering little and often, which encourages roots to rise to the surface, where they quickly dry out. You will need to water less frequently as plants mature and the roots can reach moisture at lower levels.

▲ Watering shrubs

A drip hose placed around the root area of establishing shrubs ensures that they get a thorough soaking, while reducing waste through evaporation. The hose can be disguised with a decorative mulch.

◀ Feeding shrubs

Most shrubs and climbers benefit from an annual spring feed with a slow-release fertilizer applied over the root area. Follow the application rates on the package.

Windbreaks ▶

Protect young or slightly tender plants in exposed sites with a windbreak. Fences with gaps between the panels or hedges are ideal, since they reduce the force of the wind but allow some air to pass through, which prevents turbulence behind them.

Essential pruning tips

Pruning stimulates growth and promotes new shoots and buds. Prune out dead and diseased stems first, and cut back weak growth hard and strong growth lightly. Using sharp tools, make clean, well-placed cuts (see right) that will heal quickly and reduce the risk that disease will enter.

Opposite shoots
Cut straight across these stems, just above a pair of buds or shoots.

Alternate shoots
Cut at 45°, just above the shoot, so that the lower cut is behind the bud.

Angled cut
Plants with alternate buds are pruned so that water doesn't collect on the bud.

Pruning after planting

Many deciduous shrubs respond well to being pruned just after planting. Pruning encourages more strong, healthy stems to develop and also helps to make the plant bushier. Always make your cuts just above an outward-facing bud, since this will develop into a stem that points away from the center, reducing the likelihood of crossing and congested growth. Remember that if you prune stems back hard just before a plant flowers, you will lose that year's blooms.

1 Removing dead wood
It is important to remove any dead, weak, or spindly stems by cutting them right back to the base. This encourages new shoots to grow.

2 Easing congestion
Stems that touch may create wounds that leave the plant open to disease. Prune them back to an outward-facing bud or to the ground.

3 Creating balance
Cut out stems growing at an awkward angle that spoil the shape of the plant. Try to create an evenly branching, open framework.

Pruning a climber

The same principles apply to pruning climbers as to shrubs. Some climbers, such as jasmine (see below), have a permanent framework that can be pruned in late winter or early spring to keep them in shape. Others, with more lax growth, such as late-flowering clematis, should be cut back hard in the spring. New, vigorous stems will then shoot up from the base.

1 Removing crossing stems
Prune shoots that cross or touch with sharp pruners. Cut back the wayward stems to healthy buds that are pointing in the direction you want them to grow.

2 Encouraging healthy, vigorous growth
Promote new, strong growth by pruning sideshoots back to a healthy, suitably placed bud. This can also stimulate the production of more flowering stems.

3 Removing the competition
Crowded stems at the center of a plant limit the air and light reaching the leaves, which can stunt growth and increase the likelihood that disease will take hold.

4 Providing support
Use soft twine or plastic plant ties to tie in sideshoots securely to wires or a trellis fixed to a support. Check the ties regularly and loosen as the stems thicken.

A–Z of Shrubs and Climbers

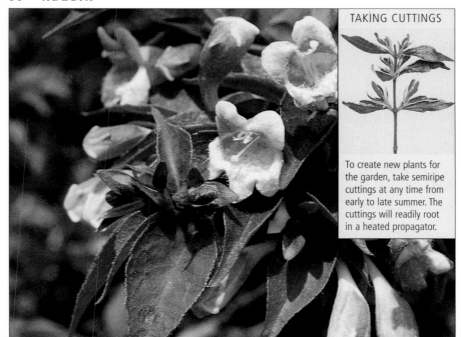

A   *Abelia schumannii*

ARCHING STEMS WITH A LATE-SEASON SHOW of 1in- (2.5cm-) long, gently scented, lilac-pink flowers make this a very useful shrub. The pinkish green outer cases, or calyces, of the flowers hang on after the blooms have dropped. To thrive, abelias need a warm, sunny position and shelter from cold winds. Prune in the spring for shape, if necessary, and to thin out old wood to prompt new growth. An excellent alternative is *Abelia* x *grandiflora* 'Francis Mason', which is slightly smaller and has yellow, variegated leaves and coppery shoots.

OTHER VARIETIES   *A.* 'Edward Goucher' (glossy, dark green leaves, bronze when young); *A. floribunda* (taller-growing, bright cerise flowers); *A.* x *grandiflora* (pink-tinged white flowers).

PLANT PROFILE
HEIGHT 6ft (2m)
SPREAD 10ft (3m)
SITE Full sun
SOIL Fertile, free-draining
HARDINESS Z7–9 H9–7
FLOWERING Late summer to autumn

Abeliophyllum distichum White forsythia

A

WITH VANILLA-SCENTED FLOWERS opening from pink buds on bare, leafless stems, this is an indispensable plant for the late winter to early spring garden. To encourage abundant flowering, grow this shrub against a sunny, sheltered wall in free-draining soil. The best time to prune is immediately after flowering has finished, which encourages plenty of the new growth that will bear next year's flowers. If you have not seen this plant before, it really does resemble a white-flowering forsythia with a pink tinge to the petals.

OTHER VARIETY *A. distichum* Roseum Group (scented, deeper pink spring flowers).

PLANT PROFILE
HEIGHT 5ft (1.5m) or more
SPREAD 5ft (1.5m)
SITE Full sun
SOIL Free-draining
HARDINESS Z5–9 H9–1
FLOWERING Late winter or early spring

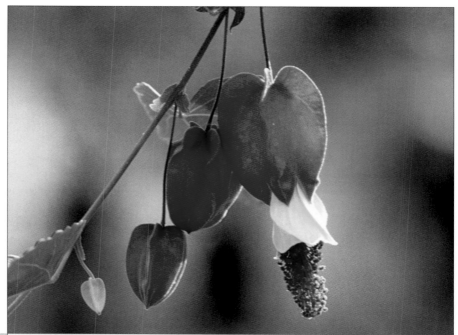

A

Abutilon megapotamicum Flowering maple

DANGLING, FLASHY, COLORFUL FLOWERS (the red part is actually the flower's outer casing) make this one of the most striking of the flowering maples. The arching, evergreen or semievergreen twiggy stems look best when arranged against a sunny, sheltered wall, or in a richly colored border. Being a native of Brazil, it will not survive wet winters, so either provide free-draining soil, or transfer it to a pot in the autumn and keep the plant in a bright, airy, frost-free place until spring.

OTHER VARIETIES *A.* 'Ashford Red' (red flowers); *A.* 'Canary Bird' (yellow flowers); *A.* 'Kentish Belle' (apricot-yellow flowers with purple stamens); *A. pictum* 'Thompsonii' (orange-flushed salmon pink flowers).

PLANT PROFILE
HEIGHT 6ft (2m)
SPREAD 6ft (2m)
SITE Full sun
SOIL Free-draining
HARDINESS Z8–10 H12–1
FLOWERING Summer to autumn

Acca sellowiana Pineapple guava

A

DON'T BE PUT OFF by this South American plant's exotic-sounding common name, because you can grow the pineapple guava in cooler regions if you provide it with a sunny, sheltered, frost-free site. It will form a good-sized shrub when planted next to a warm house wall in average to poor soil with very good drainage. The leaves are gray-green on the top surface and white underneath, while the 4in- (10cm-) wide, purple-red flowers consist of four thick, fleshy petals. With luck, after a long hot summer, you may also be rewarded with tasty, egg-shaped fruit.

OTHER VARIETY *A. sellowiana* 'Variegata' (leaves margined with creamy white).

PLANT PROFILE
HEIGHT 6ft (2m)
SPREAD 8ft (2.5m)
SITE Full sun
SOIL Free-draining
HARDINESS Z8–11 H12–9
FLOWERING Midsummer

A   *Acer negundo* 'Flamingo' Ash-leaved maple

FOR ITS FIRST 12 YEARS this deciduous tree is more like a shrub because it grows only about 1ft (30cm) taller each year. If you want to keep it at that height, prune it hard every winter—this also forces plenty of colorful, new spring growth. The shoots are red and the new leaves have attractive pink margins that then turn white, but the best effects are reserved for the autumn, when the leaves flare up with brilliant colors before falling. Promptly cut off shoots bearing all-green leaves or the whole plant may lose its variegation.

OTHER VARIETY   *A. japonicum* 'Vitifolium' (leaves turn red in autumn).

PLANT PROFILE

HEIGHT 12ft (4m) after 12 years

SPREAD 8ft (2.5m) after 12 years

SITE Full sun, partial shade

SOIL Moist, fertile, free-draining

HARDINESS Z5–8 H8–3

FLOWERING Spring

Acer palmatum 'Garnet' Japanese maple

A

THERE ARE TWO VERY GOOD REASONS for planting slow-growing Japanese maples. First, their rich autumn colors range from copper and gold to crimson and, second, they have an attractive mounded shape. 'Garnet' forms a medium-high, sprawling set of branches with finely cut leaves that turn lavish red-purple in the autumn, and hang on slightly longer than those of many other maples. All Japanese maples need a slightly sheltered site, away from cold winds and spring frosts, and acidic, rich, moist but free-draining soil.

OTHER VARIETIES *A. palmatum* 'Butterfly' (gray-green leaves margined white); *A. palmatum* var. *dissectum* (finely cut leaves turning gold in autumn); *A. palmatum* 'Osakazuki' (leaves turn brilliant red).

PLANT PROFILE
HEIGHT 25ft (8m)
SPREAD 30ft (10m)
SITE Sun or partial shade
SOIL Acidic, fertile, moist but free-draining
HARDINESS Z6–9
FLOWERING Midspring

A | *Actinidia kolomikta* Variegated kiwi vine

THIS TWINING, WOODY, DECIDUOUS CLIMBER provides lively foliage colors in the spring, plus a good autumn show. The young, heart-shaped, bronzy purple leaves are white and then pink at the tips, and at the end of the season they turn fiery red. In between, there are gently scented white flowers, but to get the small, edible, yellow-green, gooseberry-like fruit, you will need male and female plants in close proximity. Actinidia needs a position in full sun for a good display of leaf colors, and should be trained against horizontal wires on a wall. Prune for shape and to thin out the stems in late winter.

OTHER VARIETIES *A. arguta* (taller-growing, fragrant white flowers, dark green leaves); *A. deliciosa* (females produce edible fruit).

PLANT PROFILE
HEIGHT 15ft (5m)
SITE Full sun
SOIL Fertile, free-draining
HARDINESS Z5–8 H8–5
FLOWERING Early summer

Aesculus pavia 'Atrosanguinea' Red buckeye

A

TOWERING HORSE CHESTNUTS might be in this plant's genes, but red buckeye is actually a relatively modest-sized shrub or small tree. It has 5in- (13cm-) long, dangling, glossy leaves that turn gold in the autumn, and dark red, bottlebrush-like flowers, followed in autumn by smooth-skinned fruit. This is quite a large shrub, and it is best grown in wild or woodland gardens, or you could plant it as part of a perimeter garden hedge. The red buckeye likes a sunny or partially shaded site and fertile, moist but free-draining soil.

OTHER VARIETY *A. parviflora* (smaller-growing, spidery white flowers with protruding stamens).

PLANT PROFILE	
HEIGHT 15ft (5m)	
SPREAD 10ft (3m)	
SITE Sun or partial shade	
SOIL Moist, fertile, free-draining	
HARDINESS Z5–9 H9–5	
FLOWERING Early summer	

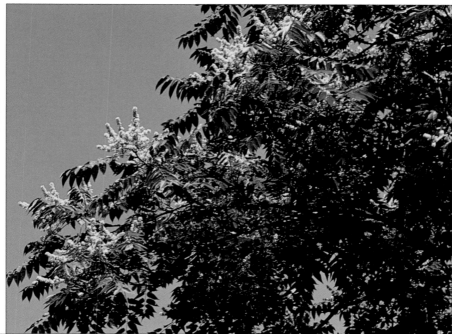

A   *Ailanthus altissima* Tree of heaven

ALTHOUGH A LARGE TREE in its native China, in gardens it does not usually become too big. The best technique for garden cultivation is to cut it back hard in late winter or early spring to just above ground level, forcing up one impressive flagpolelike stem. If other stems start growing, remove them, leaving the most vigorous to develop. It subsequently produces a few huge leaves, up to 3–4ft (90–120cm) long, which are divided into about 30 smaller leaflets, and makes a dramatic, architectural centerpiece for an unusual garden design. Alternatively, you can allow a few stems to grow, giving it a more bushlike appearance. Provide rich soil and a sheltered position to prevent the wind from ripping the foliage.

PLANT PROFILE	
HEIGHT 6–8ft (2–2.5m)	
SPREAD 50ft (15m)	
SITE Sun or partial shade	
SOIL Fertile, free-draining	
HARDINESS Z4–8 H8–1	
FLOWERING Summer	

Akebia quinata Chocolate vine

A

INTERESTING AND HIGHLY DISTINCTIVE, this semievergreen climber produces small, vanilla-scented, brownish purple flowers. The female flowers are about 1in (3cm) wide, and are larger than the adjacent males. Given a warm spring and a long, hot summer, it may produce fruit resembling a string of miniature sausages. It is a fast, sometimes invasive plant and needs rich, moist but well-drained soil. Though fairly hardy, young plants also benefit from a thick mulch of compost for protection during their first winters. Grow it along horizontal wires on a wall or sturdy fence, which it will quickly cover, and prune to control growth after flowering.

OTHER VARIETY *A. trifoliata* (hanging clusters of purple flowers).

PLANT PROFILE
HEIGHT 30ft (10m)
SITE Full sun or partial shade
SOIL Fertile, moist but free-draining
HARDINESS Z5–9 H9–5
FLOWERING Early spring

A

Aloysia triphylla Lemon verbena

STRONGLY LEMON-SCENTED, DECIDUOUS LEAVES are this plant's most desirable feature, making it a valuable, aromatic addition to an outdoor seating area. In late summer it also produces airy sprays of tiny, pale lilac to white flowers. A Mediterranean plant, it is best planted with the protection of a warm, sunny wall to reflect light and heat, and needs poor, free-draining soil. In summer borders it helps if lemon verbena is flanked by flowers with plenty of impact and color because it is grown for its scent, not its looks. It can also be potted in a large container, which can be brought into a conservatory over winter. It looks particularly striking when grown as a standard, since its leaves are then conveniently at nose level. The foliage makes an excellent ingredient in potpourri.

PLANT PROFILE	
HEIGHT 6ft (2m)	
SPREAD 6ft (2m)	
SITE Full sun	
SOIL Average, free-draining	
HARDINESS Z8–11 H12–8	
FLOWERING Late summer	

Amelanchier canadensis Shadbush

A

ERECT AND MULTISTEMMED, the shadbush is a star performer in the autumn, when the leaves turn yellow, orange, and then rich red, all at different times. The effect is a fantastic mix of colors. It also gives a good show in spring, when it bears clusters of pure white flowers, followed by blue-black berries. Grow it in a woodland or wild garden, or at the garden's edge, in acidic, moist but well-drained soil. If you have room in the garden for more than one, then try the 20ft- (6m-) high *Amelanchier x grandiflora* 'Ballerina', which has red berries that ripen to black, and equally good autumn leaf color.

OTHER VARIETY *A. lamarckii* (taller-growing, leaves colored orange and red).

PLANT PROFILE	
HEIGHT 20ft (6m)	
SPREAD 25ft (8m)	
SITE Sun or partial shade	
SOIL Acidic, fertile, moist but free-draining	
HARDINESS Z3–7 H7–1	
FLOWERING Spring	

A | *Amorpha fruticosa* Bastard indigo

THIN SPIKES HOLDING CLUSTERS of tiny purple-blue flowers, less than 1in (2.5cm) long, appear in late summer. In addition, this useful deciduous shrub has scented, 12in- (30cm-) long leaves composed of up to 33 small, oval leaflets, which make a good addition to flower arrangements. It needs light, free-draining, poor soil and thrives in difficult areas where few other shrubs will grow. Prune it in early spring, when the topgrowth should be removed, leaving the main structure of woody stems to carry the new season's leaves, stems, and flowers.

PLANT PROFILE	
HEIGHT 15ft (5m)	
SPREAD 15ft (5m)	
SITE Sun or partial shade	
SOIL Free-draining	
HARDINESS Z4–9 H9–1	
FLOWERING Late summer	

Ampelopsis glandulosa var. *brevipedunculata* 'Elegans' Porcelain vine

THIS STRIKING, ELEGANT, DECIDUOUS CLIMBER has a pleasing mix of small green leaves, splashed pink and white, with turquoise blue berries in the autumn that are fully revealed after the foliage has fallen. 'Elegans' needs free-draining soil and a warm, sunny, sheltered site against a wall for the best fruit. It also grows well over pergolas, and looks especially effective if you allow some berrying stems to dangle down. If it is being grown up a house wall, prune the topgrowth annually, ensuring that it is well clear of the gutters, which will quickly become clogged with fallen leaves.

OTHER VARIETY *A. megalophylla* (dark green leaves and green flowers followed by black fruit).

PLANT PROFILE

HEIGHT 10ft (3m)

SITE Sun or partial shade

SOIL Free-draining

HARDINESS Z6–9

FLOWERING Summer

A | *Andromeda polifolia* Common bog rosemary

THIS SMALL PLANT MAKES A MOUND of leathery, evergreen leaves, similar to those of rosemary, on wiry stems. The tiny flowers appear in compact clusters at the tips of the leafy stems. Far too small to plant near large shrubs, such as rhododendrons and camellias, it is best grown with heathers, at the front of a border, or in a raised bed or rock garden. The ideal growing conditions are moist, rich, acidic soil; if the soil is on the dry side, add a thick mulch of leaf mold in the spring after heavy rain while the soil is still very wet.

OTHER VARIETIES *A. polifolia* 'Alba' (pure white flowers); *A. polifolia* 'Compacta' (pink flowers); *A. polifolia* 'Macrophylla' (smaller-growing, deep pink and white flowers); *A. polifolia* 'Nikko' (clear pink flowers).

PLANT PROFILE
HEIGHT 16in (40cm)
SPREAD 24in (60cm)
SITE Partial shade or full sun
SOIL Acidic, moist, fertile
HARDINESS Z2–6 H6–1
FLOWERING Spring to early summer

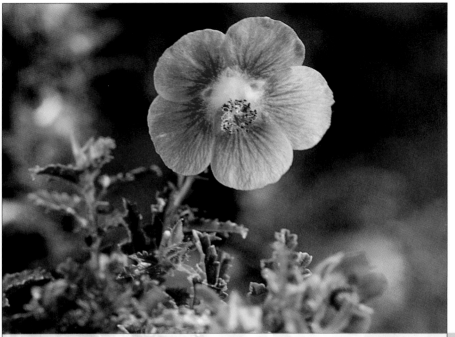

Anisodontea capensis Cape mallow

A

FIND THE WARMEST, SUNNIEST SPOT in the garden, with shelter and good drainage, for this tender South African evergreen. In frost-prone areas, it is best to grow it in a pot and bring it inside for the winter. Despite its delicate nature, it is well worth growing for its long show of 1in- (2.5cm-) wide, red-purple flowers, held on vertical, hairy stems, which last all through the summer and into the early autumn. When the shrub is young, nip out the tips of the branches to encourage more flowering stems and a bushier, denser look. Once it is established, after a few years, a gentle annual trim in mid- or late spring is all you need to do to keep it in shape.

PLANT PROFILE
HEIGHT 24–40in (60–100cm)
SPREAD 16–32in (40–80cm)
SITE Full sun
SOIL Average, free-draining
HARDINESS Z8–9 H9–8
FLOWERING Summer to autumn

A | *Antigonon leptopus* Confederate vine

UNUSUAL HEART-SHAPED FOLIAGE is the best feature of this quick-growing, South American evergreen vine. In ideal conditions it will flower over a long summer period and into the autumn, but in cooler regions it tends to flower late in the summer. The flowers typically range from coral pink to red, although they can be white. Because it needs a frost-free environment over the winter, dig it up in late autumn, cut it back, and keep it in a pot in an unheated greenhouse or on a cool windowsill, watering only occasionally to stop the soil from drying out. The following spring, stand it outside during the day, and bring it in at night until the last frost is past. Then, in early summer, you can finally plant it outside again.

PLANT PROFILE

HEIGHT 15–20ft (5–6m)

SITE Full sun

SOIL Average, free-draining

HARDINESS Z14–15 H12–10

FLOWERING Late summer

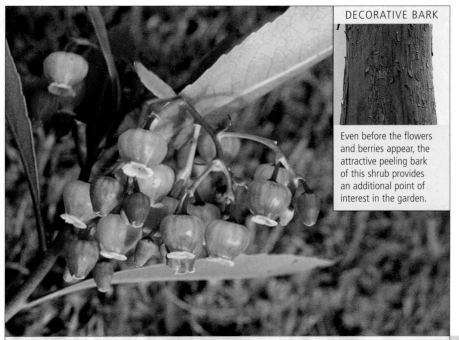

DECORATIVE BARK

Even before the flowers
and berries appear, the
attractive peeling bark
of this shrub provides
an additional point of
interest in the garden.

Arbutus unedo f. *rubra* Strawberry tree

A

TECHNICALLY A TREE, this plant is actually branching and shrubby,
and grows about 12in (30cm) a year. It has particularly attractive
shedding, reddish brown bark, and the leaves are 4in (10cm) long
and glossy. The small, dark pink flowers are followed in autumn by
bright red strawberry-like fruit, which explains the plant's common
name. In fact, the berries start to develop the previous year, and take
12 months to fatten up and ripen. Grow the strawberry tree in rich,
free-draining, acidic soil in a sheltered spot. 'Elfin King' is a compact
form, growing 6ft (2m) high and 5ft (1.5m) wide.

OTHER VARIETY *A. andrachne* (smooth, peeling, red-brown bark,
white flowers followed by orange-red berries).

PLANT PROFILE
HEIGHT 25ft (8m)
SPREAD 25ft (8m)
SITE Sun
SOIL Acidic, fertile, free-draining
HARDINESS Z8–9 H9–6
FLOWERING Autumn

A *Arctostaphylos* x *media* 'Wood's Red' Bearberry

ITS LOW MAXIMUM HEIGHT makes 'Wood's Red' an excellent plant for a rock garden or the front of a border, where it produces a show of small, rounded, evergreen leaves. It scores high points for its large, glossy red berries, which develop after the pink flowers have faded. Alternatives include 'Snow Camp', which forms a mat of stems on the ground, and has pink flowers followed by red berries, or try the white-flowered *Arctostaphylos uva-ursi* (common bearberry) which also bears scarlet berries. All need acidic, moist but well-drained soil.

OTHER VARIETY *A. uva-ursi* 'Vancouver Jade' (small pink flowers).

PLANT PROFILE

HEIGHT 4in (10cm)

SPREAD 20in (50cm) or more

SITE Full sun, partial shade

SOIL Acidic, moist but free-draining

HARDINESS Z2–6 H9–7

FLOWERING Late spring and early summer

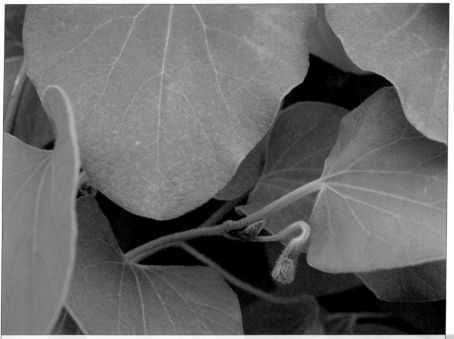

Aristolochia macrophylla Dutchman's pipe

THIS IS ONE OF THE MOST INTRIGUING climbers. It produces small, extraordinary flowers that look like a curved, ornate smoker's pipe with a U-bend in the middle, while the open end of each bloom has flared lips that are mottled in three colors. The only problem is that the flowers do become obscured by the large, heart-shaped, deciduous leaves and twisting, twining stems. This climber can be grown up a tree or trellis for support. Ensure that the soil is free-draining because Dutchman's pipe dislikes standing in wet winter soil. Protect it during the winter in colder zones with a thick mulch of compost.

PLANT PROFILE

HEIGHT	25–30ft (8–10m)
SITE	Sun or partial shade
SOIL	Fertile, free-draining
HARDINESS	Z5–8 H8–4
FLOWERING	Summer

Aronia arbutifolia Red chokeberry

THE THREE GOOD REASONS for growing *Aronia arbutifolia* are its sprays of small, white flowers (sometimes tinged with pink) in the spring, the red berries that hang on for a long time after the flowers are finished, and, finally, its wonderful autumn color—the leaves turn orange, red, and yellow before falling. Good drainage and moist soil are the main requirements for this easy-to-grow plant. After it has flowered, prune the flowered shoots back to strong buds. On mature plants, up to one-fifth of the old shoots should be cut back to the base to encourage new, vigorous growth.

OTHER VARIETIES *A. melanocarpa* (smaller-growing, autumn leaves turn purple-red); *A.* x *prunifolia* (autumn leaves turn dark purple-red).

PLANT PROFILE
HEIGHT 10ft (3m)
SPREAD 5ft (1.5m)
SITE Sun or partial shade
SOIL Moist but free-draining
HARDINESS Z5–9 H9–4
FLOWERING Late spring

Artemisia 'Powis Castle' Wormwood

A

DUE TO ITS WOODY STEMS and shrubby habit, this perennial is often regarded as a shrub. Making a leafy clump of silver-gray foliage, it can flower but rarely does so. When flowers do appear, they are yellow-tinged and insignificant, and are usually removed. The best garden position is where the foliage sets off the brighter colors of adjacent plants. Without full sun and sharp drainage, results will be poor. To promote new, vigorous growth, cut 'Powis Castle' back hard in the spring when you see new shoots appearing on the old wood.

OTHER VARIETIES *A. abrotanum* (taller, gray-green aromatic leaves); *A. absinthium* (silvery gray, silky-hairy leaves); *A. arborescens* (leaves with a fernlike appearance); *A. dracunculus* (lance-shaped, light green leaves).

PLANT PROFILE
HEIGHT 24in (60cm)
SPREAD 3ft (1m)
SITE Full sun
SOIL Free-draining
HARDINESS Z5–11 H12–3
FLOWERING Late summer

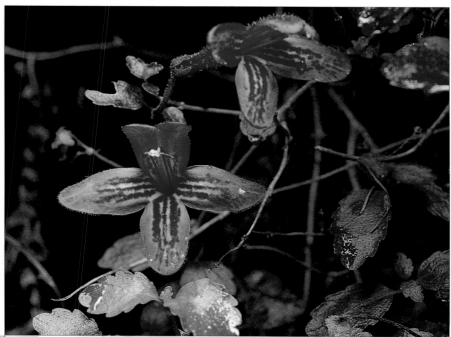

A | *Asteranthera ovata* Estrellita

IN ITS NATIVE SOUTH AMERICA, *Asteranthera ovata* may shoot up to about 4m (12ft) high, but in more temperate regions this evergreen climbing shrub will be lucky to gain a height of 45cm (18in). It will spread and creep twice this length, however, provided it is grown in moist, acidic soil and given a sheltered spot in the garden with some shade. A position at the base of a wall is ideal. In return, it produces flared, reddish pink tubular flowers, offset by small, dark green leaves on white, hairy stems. This is a quirky, highly unusual plant, and it must be given the right conditions if it is to thrive.

PLANT PROFILE

HEIGHT 18in (45cm)

SPREAD 3ft (1m)

SITE Partial shade

SOIL Acidic, moist

HARDINESS Z8–9 H9–8

FLOWERING Summer

Aucuba japonica 'Variegata' Spotted laurel

A

THESE TOTALLY RELIABLE EVERGREEN SHRUBS have a neat, solid appearance and a leafy covering from top to toe. All laurels flower, but for berries you need male and female plants. 'Variegata' is a female and gives bright red berries. Other good variegated forms include 'Gold Dust' and 'Crotonifolia', both with yellow-speckled leaves, while 'Crassifolia' is male and plain green. The all-greens are very versatile and grow happily just about anywhere, from full sun to dark shade, while the variegated types prefer dappled shade.

OTHER VARIETIES *A. japonica* f. *longifolia* 'Salicifolia' (female with slender leaves); *A. japonica* 'Picturata' (female with yellow-centered leaves); *A. japonica* 'Rozannie' (compact, dark green leaves, bisexual flowers).

PLANT PROFILE	
HEIGHT	10ft (3m)
SPREAD	10ft (3m)
SITE	Partial shade
SOIL	Average
HARDINESS	Z6–10
FLOWERING	Midspring

A | *Azara serrata* Chilean aromo

UPRIGHT AND EVERGREEN, this shrub has glossy leaves and is grown for its profuse, sweetly scented, dark yellow flowers that look like small balls of radiating bristles. In long, hot summers, the flowers are followed by tiny mauve or white berries. It is slightly tender, and is best grown against a sunny wall, where it will benefit from the extra warmth and protection, in rich, moist but free-draining soil. Prune for shape and size in late winter or early spring. *Azara microphylla* is the hardiest azara, and produces scented, greenish yellow flowers in late winter and spring—it is also happy when grown in shade.

OTHER VARIETIES *A. dentata* (fragrant, dark yellow flowers); *A. lanceolata* (lance-shaped, bright green leaves); *A. petiolaris* (leathery, dark green leaves, creamy yellow flowers in midspring).

PLANT PROFILE

HEIGHT 12ft (4m)

SPREAD 10ft (3m)

SITE Sun or partial shade

SOIL Moist, fertile, free-draining

HARDINESS Z9–11 H12–11

FLOWERING Midsummer

Ballota pseudodictamnus False dittany

B

THIS IS A KEY PLANT for gravel or Mediterranean-style gardens, and flourishes in a hot, sunny position with its roots in quite poor, free-draining soil. The stems bear small, felted, grayish yellow-green leaves, each about 1¼in (3cm) long, and end in attractive rosettes at the tips. The hotter the summer, the more felted the leaves become. Grow it in free-draining soil with some shelter from frost. In midsummer, cut back the entire plant, and it will quickly produce a fresh batch of leaves that last through the winter.

OTHER VARIETIES *B. acetabulosa* (taller-growing, small, purple-pink flowers with white marks); *B.* 'All Hallows Green' (woolly, lime green leaves, small, pale green flowers in mid- and late summer).

PLANT PROFILE
HEIGHT 18in (45cm)
SPREAD 24in (60cm)
SITE Full sun
SOIL Free-draining
HARDINESS Z7–9 H9–7
FLOWERING Late spring and early summer

B *Berberidopsis corallina* Coral plant

THIS WOODY, EVERGREEN, SCRAMBLING CLIMBER from Chile is ideal for a sheltered wall, out of direct sunlight, where it will not be flayed by cold winds. The dark green leaves grow up to 4in (10cm) long, and nicely set off the tiny, pearl-like, dark red flowers that dangle like cherries. It is slightly fussy in its requirements and needs humus-rich soil, while the roots demand a thick mulch of compost for protection in winter. This is not a vigorous climber, and it needs to be trained against horizontal wires attached to a supporting surface, although you can also encourage it to scramble up a sturdy old tree. Prune in the spring to thin out congested growth.

PLANT PROFILE

HEIGHT 15ft (5m)

SITE Partial shade

SOIL Moist, free-draining

HARDINESS Z8–9 H9–8

FLOWERING Summer to early autumn

Berberis darwinii Darwin's barberry

B

A HIGH-QUALITY EVERGREEN, this barberry puts on a show of bright orange flowers early in the year, followed by a mass of blue-black berries in the autumn. It makes a prickly, medium-high hedge or divider within the garden, growing about 12in (30cm) in height each year. For a hedge, plant the shrubs about 18in (45cm) apart. Like most barberries, *Berberis darwinii* grows just about anywhere in the garden, except on clay. Prune for shape only immediately after flowering.

OTHER VARIETIES *B.* 'Goldilocks' (red-stalked, golden yellow flowers); *B.* x *lologensis* 'Apricot Queen' (dark orange flowers); *B.* 'Red Jewel' (dark bronze-red young leaves, yellow flowers).

PLANT PROFILE
HEIGHT 10ft (3m)
SPREAD 10ft (3m)
SITE Full sun or partial shade
SOIL Free-draining
HARDINESS Z7–9 H9–7
FLOWERING Mid- and late spring

B | *Berberis thunbergii* 'Bagatelle' Japanese barberry

FOR THE FRONT OF A BORDER this barberry is hard to beat. The pale yellow flowers are followed by shiny red berries, and in the autumn the leaves flare orange and red. 'Bagatelle' is small and compact, and produces a good effect when grown beside a path, or alternated with boxwood balls or oval, evergreen, dwarf conifers. It needs only an occasional trim in late winter to keep it in shape, but beware of the spiny stems when pruning. For the best leaf color, flowering, and berrying, grow it in full sun and free-draining soil.

OTHER VARIETIES *B. thunbergii* f. *atropurpurea* (red-purple foliage, turning red in autumn); *B. thunbergii* 'Atropurpurea Nana' (red-purple foliage); *B. thunbergii* 'Rose Glow' (white-flecked, red-purple foliage).

PLANT PROFILE

HEIGHT 12in (30cm)

SPREAD 16in (40cm)

SITE Full sun

SOIL Free-draining

HARDINESS Z5–8 H8–3

FLOWERING Spring

Bignonia capreolata Cross vine

B

ALTHOUGH MAGNIFICENT AND RAMPANT, this rapid climber is on the tender side. In ideal conditions—a sunny, sheltered, frost-free site with free-draining soil, where its roots are not locked in cold, wet soil all winter—cross vine will produce large, evergreen leaves. Enclosed city gardens often provide a suitable environment. The bright, orange-red, trumpet-shaped flowers are small yet highly attractive. The tendrils need some form of support to latch on to, and this can be provided by horizontal wires attached to a wall, or by a host tree with twiggy growth at the bottom. Cross vine can also be grown in a conservatory, but you need to make sure there is a long stretch of wall for it to colonize.

PLANT PROFILE

HEIGHT 30ft (10m)

SITE Full sun

SOIL Free-draining

HARDINESS Z6–9 H9–5

FLOWERING Summer

B

Billardiera longiflora Purple apple berry

SUITABLE ONLY FOR MILD GARDENS, this small, unusual, eye-catching Australian climber never becomes too rampant. Its best feature is its liberal covering of electric blue-purple berries in early autumn, although sometimes berries can also be purple, red, pink, or white. It needs to be grown in a sunny, sheltered part of the garden, ideally against a wall, and in free-draining soil to prevent the stem from rotting in winter. If you have sufficient space for it in a warm conservatory, the display of flowers and berries will be even better. In the garden, allow its wiry stems to sprint over adjoining plants.

OTHER VARIETY *B. scandens* (bell-shaped greenish yellow or violet to purple flowers, followed by olive green berries).

PLANT PROFILE
HEIGHT 6–10ft (2–3m)
SITE Sun or partial shade
SOIL Free-draining
HARDINESS Z8–9 H9–8
FLOWERING Summer

Bomarea caldasii Climbing alstromeria

B

THIS TENDER, DECIDUOUS CLIMBER comes from South America and needs to be grown either in a conservatory or in a warm, sheltered, frost-free spot outdoors. When happy, it produces clusters of flowers, each like a small tube. The blooms are dark reddish terracotta on the outside and orange-yellow with scores of tiny spots inside. It needs moist but well-drained soil, and some protection over winter to keep off the rain. In late winter, cut back to ground level all dead topgrowth and stems that have flowered. *B. hirtella* also requires a frost-free site, and flowers well.

OTHER VARIETIES *B. hirtella* (orange-green flowers); *B. salsilla* (hardier, reddish green flowers).

PLANT PROFILE
HEIGHT 10–12ft (3–4m)
SITE Full sun
SOIL Moist but free-draining
HARDINESS Z11–15 H12–10
FLOWERING Late spring to autumn

B

Brachyglottis (Dunedin Group) 'Sunshine' Senecio

MAKING A PLUMP, EVERGREEN, SPRAWLING mound of silver-gray leaves with white hairs underneath when young, 'Sunshine' thrives in free-draining soil, especially in coastal sites. In summer it is richly colored with a bold show of yellow flowers, and can be pruned after flowering to give it a good shape and to prevent it from running into neighboring plants. Where wind protection is required, you can plant several shrubs to make a highly effective hedge. It can also be used as a contrast for adjacent climbers, such as a clematis with red flowers, which will stand out against the yellow.

OTHER VARIETIES *B. compacta* (compact, mound-forming); *B. monroi* (densely growing, leathery, olive green leaves).

PLANT PROFILE
HEIGHT 3–5ft (1–1.5m)
SPREAD 6ft (2m) or more
SITE Partial shade
SOIL Free-draining
HARDINESS Z9–10 H10–9
FLOWERING Early to midsummer

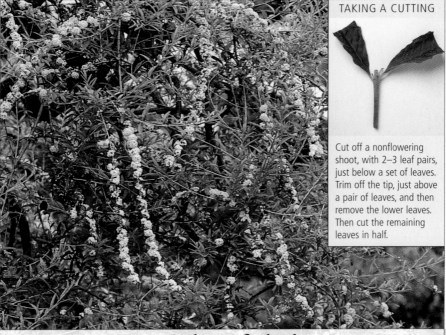

TAKING A CUTTING

Cut off a nonflowering shoot, with 2–3 leaf pairs, just below a set of leaves. Trim off the tip, just above a pair of leaves, and then remove the lower leaves. Then cut the remaining leaves in half.

Buddleja alternifolia Fountain butterfly bush

B

THIS IS A BUDDLEJA WITH A DIFFERENCE because it can be trained as a single-stem shrub, with a mass of weeping branches bearing lilac flowers growing from the top. Set it apart from other plants so that it can be better appreciated. You can also grow it in the traditional way, as a dense, deciduous shrub, or site it against a wall. The arching stems give it an elegant look, and the richly scented flowers attract bees and butterflies. Deadhead and prune after flowering, removing one-fourth of the stems. It does best on free-draining or chalky soil.

OTHER VARIETIES *B. davidii* 'Fascinating' (lilac-pink flowers); *B.* 'Lochinch' (later-flowering, orange-eyed, violet-blue flowers).

PLANT PROFILE	
HEIGHT 12ft (4m)	
SPREAD 12ft (4m)	
SITE Full sun	
SOIL Free-draining	
HARDINESS Z6–9 H10–1	
FLOWERING Early summer	

Buddleja davidii 'Black Knight' Butterfly bush

FLOWERING IN MID- AND LATE SUMMER, 'Black Knight' puts on an astonishing show of dark purple-blue flowers with a heavy, fragrant scent. Never neat and tidy, stems shoot out in different directions, especially after a spring pruning. If you deadhead it promptly, there may be a second flush of smaller flowers. This deciduous shrub likes free-draining soil and is virtually indestructible, self-seeding on any patch of poor soil. If space permits, it makes a fine contrast beside the equally vigorous *Buddleja davidii* 'White Profusion'.

OTHER VARIETIES *B. davidii* 'Dartmoor' (reddish purple flowers); *B. davidii* 'Harlequin' (red-purple flowers, cream-margined leaves); *B. davidii* 'White Bouquet' (white flowers with a yellow eye).

PLANT PROFILE	
HEIGHT 10ft (3m)	
SPREAD 15ft (5m)	
SITE Full sun	
SOIL Poor, free-draining	
HARDINESS Z6–9 H9–1	
FLOWERING Summer to autumn	

Buddleja globosa Orange ball tree

A DISTINCTIVE DECIDUOUS OR SEMIEVERGREEN shrub, this buddleja has early summer flowers that resemble small, orange golf balls, and is best grown in a sheltered site where you can really appreciate their scent. After flowering, remove the spent blooms and the top 3in (8cm) of stems, plus any wayward growth, but keep pruning to a minimum or you will lose the following year's flowers. You can use the orange ball tree as a support for annual climbers, which will disguise the bare stems that can form at the base. Alternatively, place it toward the back of a border where these stems cannot be seen.

PLANT PROFILE	
HEIGHT 15ft (5m)	
SPREAD 15ft (5m)	
SITE Full sun	
SOIL Free-draining	
HARDINESS Z7–9 H9–7	
FLOWERING Early summer	

B

Bupleurum fruticosum Shrubby hare's ear

THIS SOUND, RELIABLE CHOICE for coastal gardens makes a medium-sized, dense, rounded, evergreen shrub with 3in- (8cm-) long, blue-tinged leaves and sprays of tiny yellow flowers. Its main use is as a background linking shrub rather than as a star performer. Shrubby hare's ear requires a sunny, sheltered position where it will not be subjected to hard frosts, but it is not very fussy about the soil, provided it is free-draining. Lightly prune for shape in midspring, but if it does become overgrown and shapeless, cut it back hard at the same time of year.

OTHER VARIETY *B. angulosum* (smaller-growing, yellow or creamy green flowers surrounded by jade green bracts).

PLANT PROFILE
HEIGHT 6ft (2m)
SPREAD 8ft (2.5m)
SITE Full sun
SOIL Free-draining
HARDINESS Z7–11 H12–7
FLOWERING Midsummer to early autumn

BOX SUCKER

In midspring, infestations of flattened, pale green, aphidlike, sap-sucking insects appear and cause leaves to curl, creating stunted, cabbagelike growth. Spray or remove the affected stems.

Buxus sempervirens 'Latifolia Maculata' Common boxwood

B

ONE OF THE BEST SHRUBS for edging and topiary, common boxwood can be pruned to create a wide range of shapes—from geometric pyramids and squares to animal forms—as well as low hedges for a knot garden or parterre. 'Latifolia Maculata' is an attractive variety, with bright yellow early summer foliage that turns a darker green with yellow markings as the season advances. Old plants can be rejuvenated very easily by pruning hard in spring, while hedging and edging should be trimmed in the summer. Fertilize in spring, and water young plants well during dry spells.

OTHER VARIETIES *B. sempervirens* 'Elegantissima' (white-margined leaves); *B. sempervirens* 'Suffruticosa' (compact, good for low hedges).

PLANT PROFILE

HEIGHT	8ft (2.5m)
SPREAD	6ft (2m)
SITE	Partial shade
SOIL	Fertile, free-draining
HARDINESS	Z5–9
FLOWERING	Late spring

C | *Caesalpina pulcherrima* Barbados pride

GIVEN A SUNNY, SHELTERED SITE, Barbados pride is quite a beauty, but it can be tricky to grow because it will die if touched by frost. It produces bright green, feathery foliage that hangs on throughout the winter, provided it is kept in a warm environment. If you do grow this shrub outside, dig it up and bring it indoors in a large pot as soon as nighttime temperatures approach freezing in the autumn; alternatively, treat it as a conservatory plant. Moving it indoors for winter means that it will never grow large, but you will be compensated by the hint of exotica it brings to the garden in the summer. Give it a gentle trim after flowering, if required.

OTHER VARIETY *C. gilliesii* (smaller-growing, yellow flowers).

PLANT PROFILE
HEIGHT 10–20ft (3–6m)
SPREAD 6–12ft (2–4m)
SITE Full sun
SOIL Moist, fertile, free-draining
HARDINESS Z9–11 H12–9
FLOWERING Spring to autumn

Callicarpa bodinieri var. *giraldii* 'Profusion' Beautyberry

C

THERE IS A PURPLE–MAUVE FLASH OF COLOR just before the leaves fall in autumn, when the branches are studded with violet, pearl-like berries that persist into winter. They make this a star performer for the late-season garden. 'Profusion' also gets off to a lively start in spring with new bronze-colored leaves that turn green over the summer. An erect shrub, 'Profusion' has stiff woody stems, and likes free-draining soil. To keep it vigorous and free-berrying, prune one in five stems to the ground each spring to encourage new growth.

OTHER VARIETIES *C. bodinieri* var. *giraldii* (pink flowers, dark green leaves); *C. dichotoma* (smaller-growing, pale pink flowers followed by dark lilac fruit); *C. japonica* 'Leucocarpa' (white flowers and fruit).

PLANT PROFILE		
HEIGHT 10ft (3m)		
SPREAD 8ft (2.5m)		
SITE Full sun or dappled shade		
SOIL Free-draining		
HARDINESS Z4–7 H7–1		
FLOWERING Midsummer		

C

Callistemon citrinus 'Splendens' Crimson bottlebrush

AUSTRALIAN BOTTLEBRUSHES ARE FUN PLANTS, making large shrubs with cylindrical, tactile flowers consisting of scores of bristlelike stamens. Their hardiness varies, and this evergreen belongs to the tender category. It can be grown and kept small in a pot, which should be brought into a conservatory or heated greenhouse over winter. It needs free-draining, moderately fertile, neutral to acidic soil, and can be pruned lightly after flowering to give an attractive shape, although you can be more ruthless in spring if it grows too large. For a permanent border plant, try the hardier *C. subulatus*.

OTHER VARIETIES *C. pallidus* (smaller-growing, greenish yellow flowers); *C. salignus* (white flowers); *C. sieberi* (creamy yellow flowers).

PLANT PROFILE
HEIGHT 6–25ft (2–8m)
SPREAD 5–20ft (1.5–6m)
SITE Full sun
SOIL Free-draining
HARDINESS Z12–15 H12–10
FLOWERING Spring and summer

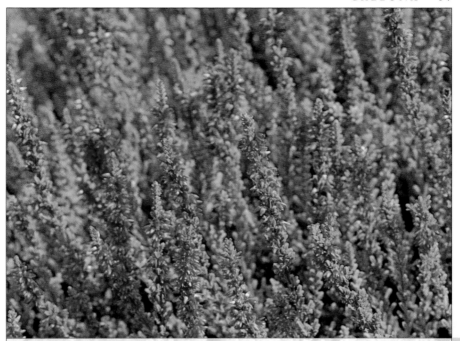

Calluna vulgaris 'Firefly' Scotch heather

C

THE PERFECT PLACE for growing evergreen heathers is in a border with acidic soil. 'Firefly' has terracotta-colored leaves in the summer; they turn dark brick red over winter. It mixes well with golden yellow 'Sir John Charrington', which has orange and red winter foliage, and copper-red 'Glenfiddich', which turns bronze-red when temperatures fall. If the height of heathers is too uniform, combine them with conifers for variety. All callunas are easy to grow in rich, free-draining soil, and will need just a gentle trim in early spring, although excessively long leaves can be snipped off at any time.

OTHER VARIETIES *C. vulgaris* 'Beoley Silver' (silver foliage, white flowers); *C. vulgaris* 'Darkness' (crimson flowers).

PLANT PROFILE
HEIGHT 18in (45cm)
SPREAD 30in (75cm)
SITE Full sun
SOIL Acidic, fertile, free-draining
HARDINESS Z5–7 H7–5
FLOWERING Midsummer to late autumn

C

Calycanthus floridus Carolina allspice

FOR ANY SCENTED GARDEN, the deciduous Carolina allspice is an important component. It emits a rich, fruity scent from its leaves (when rubbed), bark, and small, dark red flowers. The blooms also resemble waterlilies, while the attractive dark green leaves are covered with downy wool beneath, and turn yellow before falling in the autumn. Make sure that the soil is moist and rich, and for the best results provide a warm, sheltered site. Prune in early spring by cutting back hard to the base framework of oldest wood in order to prompt new, vigorous growth.

OTHER VARIETY *C. occidentalis* (red flowers with brown-tipped petals).

PLANT PROFILE
HEIGHT 8ft (2.5m)
SPREAD 10ft (3m)
SITE Sun
SOIL Moist, fertile
HARDINESS Z5–9 H9–1
FLOWERING Summer

Camellia x *williamsii* 'Donation'

C

ONE OF THE MOST VERSATILE CAMELLIAS, this is a tough, erect shrub with an eye-catching show of semidouble pink flowers that are even darker and longer-lasting when grown in partial shade. Like all camellias, it needs a sheltered position away from cold winds and from the early morning sun so that frosted flower buds thaw slowly and are not damaged. Camellias also require acidic soil, which should be mulched with compost to stop it from drying out.

OTHER VARIETIES *C. japonica* 'Bob's Tinsie' (small, brilliant red flowers); *C. japonica* 'Elegans' (large, rose pink flowers); *C. sasanqua* 'Narumigata' (pink-tinged white flowers); *C.* x *williamsii* 'Anticipation' (very large crimson flowers); *C.* x *williamsii* 'St Ewe' (rose pink flowers).

PLANT PROFILE	
HEIGHT 15ft (5m)	
SPREAD 8ft (2.5m)	
SITE Light shade	
SOIL Acidic, moist, fertile, free-draining	
HARDINESS Z7–8 H8–7	
FLOWERING Late winter to late spring	

C | *Campsis* x *tagliabuana* 'Madame Galen' Trumpet vine

IF YOU HAVE A SUNNY, SHELTERED WALL then this deciduous climber will erupt with richly colored, trumpet-shaped flowers, about 9in (23cm) long. The warmer and more sheltered its position, the better, because 'Madame Galen' needs a long, hot summer to excel. Naturally vigorous, it requires poor to average soil, which must not dry out over summer. Cutting back young climbers just after planting, leaving just 8in (20cm) of growth, forces them to produce new, bushy stems, while established plants can be pruned hard in late winter, cutting back sideshoots to leave just three buds at the base.

OTHER VARIETIES   *C. grandiflora* (dark orange to red flowers); *C. radicans* f. *flava* (yellow flowers).

PLANT PROFILE
HEIGHT 30ft (10m)
SITE Full sun
SOIL Average, moist
HARDINESS Z5–9 H9–5
FLOWERING Late summer to autumn

Cantua buxifolia Sacred flower of the Incas

C

THIS EXOTIC SOUTH AMERICAN PLANT is a tender shrub with quite specific growing requirements. It needs a hot, sunny position, rich, moist but well-drained soil, and protection from cold winds, but find the right spot and you will be rewarded in spring with a liberal covering of dangling, tubular, fuchsialike, pink to purple flowers. If you don't have the right conditions in the garden, it can be grown in a conservatory and trained against a wall for support. The best time to prune it is after flowering, when it needs just a light trim to maintain its shape and restrict it to the available space.

PLANT PROFILE

HEIGHT 6–15ft (2–5m)

SPREAD 5–8ft (1.5–2.5m)

SITE Full sun

SOIL Fertile, moist but free-draining

HARDINESS Z10–11 H12–10

FLOWERING Spring

C | *Carpenteria californica* Bush anemone

THIS SUPERB EVERGREEN has papery, peeling, beige-colored bark
and glossy, leathery leaves up to 5in (12cm) long. In early summer
there is an arresting show of circular, gently scented white flowers
with yellow centers. It needs to bask in the warmest, most sheltered
part of the garden in free-draining soil. 'Ladhams' Variety' has
slightly larger white flowers, up to 3in (8cm) wide, while the more
compact 'Elizabeth' has smaller ones. Prune after flowering, if
necessary, to maintain its shape.

OTHER VARIETY *C. californica* 'Bodnant' (flowers and leaves similar
to *C. californica*, but hardier).

PLANT PROFILE
HEIGHT 6ft (2m) or more
SPREAD 6ft (2m)
SITE Full sun
SOIL Free-draining
HARDINESS Z8–9 H9–8
FLOWERING Early and midsummer

Caryopteris x *clandonensis* 'Heavenly Blue' Bluebeard

C

THE RICH BLUE FLOWERS on erect stems bring the front or middle of a border to life in the second half of summer. The gray–green leaves, silvery beneath, of this bushy deciduous shrub release a pungent scent if rubbed, and make a wonderful foil for the flowers. Where growing a couple, include 'Dark Knight' with its silvery leaves and dark blue flowers. Caryopteris looks good against gravel, and thrive in sunny gardens with well-drained soil. In mid- to late spring, cut back the stems to within a few buds of the main framework.

OTHER VARIETIES *C.* x *clandonensis* 'Kew Blue' (dark blue flowers, gray-green leaves); *C.* x *clandonensis* 'Worcester Gold' (yellow leaves, pale blue flowers); *C. incana* (bright violet-blue, sometimes white, flowers).

PLANT PROFILE
HEIGHT 3ft (1m)
SPREAD 3ft (1m)
SITE Full sun
SOIL Free-draining
HARDINESS Z6–9 H9–4
FLOWERING Late summer and early autumn

C | *Cassiope* 'Edinburgh'

SMALL AND EVERGREEN, this front-of-border shrub has wiry stems with scalelike, dark green leaves and small, delicate-looking, bell-shaped white flowers. It is suitable for a rock garden, or plant it beneath trees in a woodland-style setting, but in both cases ensure that the soil is acidic and moist. The site must be sheltered if cassiope is to thrive. *Cassiope lycopodioides* also has white flowers, but is even shorter, reaching just 3in (8cm) high, with a spreading habit.

OTHER VARIETIES *C. lycopodioides* 'Beatrice Lilley' (dwarf, compact variety); *C.* 'Muirhead' (white flowers, silvery leaves).

PLANT PROFILE	
HEIGHT To 10in (25cm)	
SPREAD To 10in (25cm)	
SITE Partial shade or sun	
SOIL Acidic, moist	
HARDINESS Z2–6 H6–1	
FLOWERING Late spring	

Ceanothus 'Blue Mound' California lilac

GIVEN THE RIGHT CONDITIONS, some California lilacs make massive plants, typically with a covering of blue flowers, although they also come in pink and white. This medium-high evergreen shrub forms a mound and has dark green leaves. It needs sun, shelter, and free-draining soil—for example, against a wall in a gravel garden. Prune after flowering, either lightly or, if overgrown, by cutting back the flowered shoots by one-third to one-half. Young plants benefit from a thick winter mulch of compost in their first few years.

OTHER VARIETIES *C.* 'Autumnal Blue' (taller, sky blue flowers); *C.* 'Burkwoodii' (later-flowering, bright blue flowers); *C.* 'Cascade' (powder blue flowers); *C.* 'Southmead' (dark, rich blue flowers).

PLANT PROFILE

HEIGHT 5ft (1.5m)

SPREAD 6ft (2m)

SITE Full sun

SOIL Free-draining

HARDINESS Z9–10 H10–8

FLOWERING Late spring

C

Celastrus orbiculatus Oriental bittersweet

THIS DECIDUOUS, RAMPANT, TWINING CLIMBER needs a large, strong structure to romp up—a wall, well-built pergola, or sturdy tree are all good options. The summer flowers are quite small and not especially noteworthy, but the seed capsules are a real bonus. They are yellow, like the leaves when they change color in the autumn, and split open to reveal tiny seeds that are usually pink or orange-red. The capsules have a huge visual impact in the autumn, and although separate male and female plants are required to get to this stage, some nurseries offer Hermaphrodite Group plants, which produce seed without a partner. Grow these plants in free-draining soil, in either full sun or partial shade.

PLANT PROFILE

HEIGHT 45ft (14m)

SITE Full sun, partial shade

SOIL Free-draining

HARDINESS Z4–8 H8–1

FLOWERING Summer

Ceratostigma willmottianum Chinese plumbago

C

OF ALL THE TYPES OF PLUMBAGO, this is the hardiest and best choice. A deciduous, vigorous shrub, in late summer it is liberally covered in mid-blue flowers that are offset by red-tinted autumn foliage. Cold winters can cause the stems to die back, but if you prune it down to the ground in spring, it quickly rejuvenates, sending up dozens of new stems. To help it survive cold winters, make sure that the soil is free-draining, because the roots hate being locked in wet soil, and give it a sunny, protected position.

OTHER VARIETIES *C. griffithii* (red-stemmed, mid-green leaves with purple margins); *C. plumbaginoides* (smaller-growing, spikes of brilliant blue flowers).

PLANT PROFILE	
HEIGHT 3ft (1m)	
SPREAD 5ft (1.5m)	
SITE Full sun	
SOIL Free-draining	
HARDINESS Z6–9 H9–6	
FLOWERING Late summer and autumn	

C

Cercis canadensis 'Forest Pansy' Eastern redbud

STRICTLY SPEAKING, THIS IS A SPREADING TREE, but in its early years 'Forest Pansy' has very shrubby growth. The leaves are its most impressive feature. Heart-shaped and rich reddish purple, they add a dash of color in summer. Because they look particularly bright when backlit, place them where the sun is behind them for part of the day. If the plant grows too large, prune it back annually to near ground level, leaving just 2–3 buds at the base, or cut off the crown where most of the stems meet the trunk (known as pollarding) in early spring. These pruning methods also produce the best show of leaves.

OTHER VARIETIES *C. canadensis* (bronze leaves turning yellow in autumn); *C. chinensis* (smaller-growing, green leaves turning yellow).

PLANT PROFILE
HEIGHT 30ft (10m)
SPREAD 30ft (10m)
SITE Full sun or dappled shade
SOIL Moist, fertile, free-draining
HARDINESS Z6–9 H9–6
FLOWERING Spring

Cestrum parqui Willow–leaved jasmine

C

THE BEST REASON for growing the sweetly scented willow-leaved jasmine is that you can place it close to outdoor dining areas. It does not look particularly exotic—in fact, the flowers are a pallid yellow-green—but this plant is definitely on the tender side. Provide it with a sunny, sheltered spot in the garden, and rich, free-draining soil. If the topgrowth does die back during a hard winter, new shoots should emerge from the base in the following spring.

OTHER VARIETIES   *C. fasciculatum* (bright red flowers, dark green, wavy-edged leaves); *C.* 'Newellii' (taller-growing, crimson flowers often followed by purple-red berries).

PLANT PROFILE
HEIGHT 6ft (2m)
SPREAD 6ft (2m)
SITE Sun or partial shade
SOIL Fertile, free-draining
HARDINESS Z8–11 H12–8
FLOWERING Summer to autumn

C | *Chaenomeles* x *superba* 'Pink Lady' Flowering quince

ONE OF THE BEST SIGHTS in the spring garden is a wall-trained quince with stiff, bare, woody stems and dark pink flowers. Alternatively, you can grow it as a tangled, freestanding bush. It will be happy in average soil, and does well in shade or sun, although it will flower and fruit better in a light position. 'Fire Dance' is good companion plant because it adds bright red flowers to the pink. If you are growing it against a wall, use the stems as a sturdy support for a flowering clematis, which will happily clamber up through it.

OTHER VARIETIES *C. speciosa* 'Moerloosei' (white flowers, flushed pink); *C.* x *superba* 'Crimson and Gold' (compact, dark red flowers with yellow centers); *C.* x *superba* 'Knap Hill Scarlet' (large red flowers).

PLANT PROFILE
HEIGHT 5ft (1.5m)
SPREAD 6ft (2m)
SITE Sun or light shade
SOIL Average, free-draining
HARDINESS Z5–8 H9–4
FLOWERING Spring

Chimonanthus praecox Wintersweet

C

THIS MUST-HAVE PLANT for the second half of winter has spicy-scented, bell-shaped, lemon yellow flowers, 1in (2.5cm) wide, that appear on the bare stems. Don't despair if a new plant does not flower in its first winter—it may take up to five years to bloom. While it makes a vigorous, freestanding shrub, it will grow taller against a sunny wall, where it also benefits from the extra shelter and warmth. Plant it in moderately fertile, free-draining soil and prune the flowered stems of wall-trained plants immediately after blooming, leaving just three leaves on each.

OTHER VARIETIES *C. praecox* 'Grandiflorus'(deep yellow flowers with maroon stripes inside); *C. praecox* var. 'Luteus' (yellow, wide flowers).

PLANT PROFILE
HEIGHT 12ft (4m)
SPREAD 10ft (3m)
SITE Full sun
SOIL Free-draining
HARDINESS Z7–9 H9–7
FLOWERING Winter

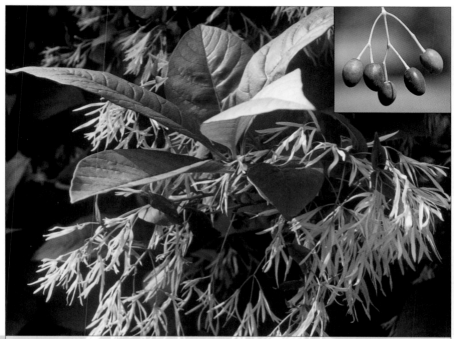

C *Chionanthus virginicus* Fringe tree

THIS ATTRACTIVE, DECIDUOUS SHRUB or small tree has large, glossy, dark green leaves that turn yellow in the autumn before falling. The fringe tree deserves to be far more popular than it is, not least for its gently scented, wispy white flowers, which are followed, with luck, by small, blue-black fruit. The longer and hotter the summer, the better the display is likely to be. It is easy to grow, and likes free-draining soil and a sunny position. Prune the fringe tree in the late winter or early spring, when necessary, to maintain its shape or size.

OTHER VARIETY *C. retusus* (peeling or deeply furrowed bark, fragrant white flowers).

PLANT PROFILE
HEIGHT 10ft (3m)
SPREAD 10ft (3m) or more
SITE Full sun
SOIL Fertile, free-draining
HARDINESS Z4–9 H9–1
FLOWERING Summer

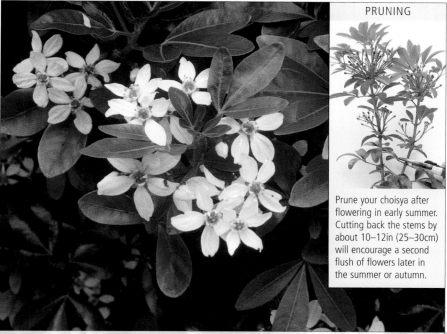

Prune your choisya after flowering in early summer. Cutting back the stems by about 10–12in (25–30cm) will encourage a second flush of flowers later in the summer or autumn.

Choisya ternata Mexican orange blossom

C

THIS FABULOUS EVERGREEN has fingerlike foliage and is studded with open, scented, starry white blooms. The main burst of flowers appears in late spring but, especially in warm, sheltered sites, it will bloom again later in the year. Mexican orange blossom is a rounded shrub, requiring only occasional pruning to keep it neat. It looks particularly good when planted with *Crocosmia* 'Lucifer' spearing its tomato red flowers up through the front of the shrub, and if you grow it against a sunny, sheltered wall, the rich, sweet scent of the flowers will linger in the air.

OTHER VARIETIES   *C.* 'Aztec Pearl' (pink-tinged white flowers); *C. ternata* 'Sundance' (bright yellow young leaves, white flowers).

PLANT PROFILE

HEIGHT To 8ft (2.5m)

SPREAD To 8ft (2.5m)

SITE Full sun

SOIL Fertile, free-draining

HARDINESS Z8–10 H10–8

FLOWERING Late spring, and again, with fewer flowers, in summer and autumn

C | *Chusquea culeou* Chilean straight bamboo

YOU WILL NEED A BIG GARDEN to accommodate this big, thicket-forming bamboo. It makes an incredibly impressive clump when growing out of its own bed in the middle of a lawn, looking like it has erupted out of the ground. It prefers rich soil and needs to be watered well during its first season to help it develop a good root system, but never plant it close to a pond, especially one with an artificial sheet lining, or the new canes may spear up through the base and cause a leak. If new canes emerge too far from the clump, slice them off at ground level with a spade. Old canes can be sawed off in the spring, just below the surface to prevent the stumps from protruding, while occasional pruning allows air and light into the center of the clump. Treat with a general fertilizer in the spring.

PLANT PROFILE
HEIGHT 20ft (6m)
SPREAD 8ft (2.5m)
SITE Sun or partial shade
SOIL Fertile
HARDINESS Z8–13 H12–10

Cistus x *argenteus* 'Peggy Sammons' Rock rose

SUN-LOVING AND STRONG-GROWING, this evergreen rock rose gives an excellent show of dark pink flowers all summer. Each flower lasts only one day, if that, but is replaced by others in rapid succession. 'Peggy Sammons' thrives in hot sun in poor, sandy soil with good drainage, and needs shelter from cold winter winds. In colder zones, provide a thick, protective winter mulch of compost. It is a short-lived plant and needs replacing every few years, or you can take cuttings in the early summer.

OTHER VARIETIES *C.* x *corbariensis* (white flowers from red buds); *C. ladanifer* (taller-growing, white flowers); *C.* x *pulverulentus* 'Sunset' (rose pink flowers with yellow centers); *C.* x *skanbergii* (pink flowers).

PLANT PROFILE
HEIGHT 3ft (1m)
SPREAD 3ft (1m)
SITE Full sun
SOIL Poor, free-draining
HARDINESS Z8–10 H10–8
FLOWERING Summer

C | *Clematis alpina* 'Frances Rivis'

FEATURING NODDING, MID-BLUE FLOWERS, 3in (8cm) wide, followed by fluffy seedheads, this exquisite climber gives any spring garden a graceful lift. It tolerates exposed sites, and makes a beautiful contrast when trained through a pink or red flowering quince (*Chaenomeles*) that flowers at the same time. The roots like shaded, moist, rich soil, while the flowers prefer to have their heads in the sun. Plant all clematis with the root ball 3in (8cm) below soil level to safeguard against disease and to promote strong, new shoots low down.

OTHER VARIETY *C. macropetala* (blue or violet-blue flowers).

PLANT PROFILE
HEIGHT 10ft (3m)
SPREAD 5ft (1.5m)
SITE Full sun
SOIL Moist, fertile
HARDINESS Z6–9 H9–6
FLOWERING Mid- to late spring

Clematis armandii 'Apple Blossom'

C

THERE ARE TWO GOOD REASONS for growing this plant: it produces pink-tinged flowers with a scent of vanilla, and has evergreen, long, dark green leaves. Plant it in a sheltered, sunny position to prevent the young bronze leaves from being ruined, or even killed, by cold winds, and to protect the flower buds from frost damage. A sheltered site also ensures that the flower scent lingers in the air. The roots need to be in shaded, moist, rich soil, and the flowers in the sun. Prune to keep it in check immediately after flowering.

OTHER VARIETY *C. alpina* (blue flowers followed by fluffy seedheads).

PLANT PROFILE

HEIGHT 15ft (5m)

SPREAD 10ft (3m)

SITE Full sun

SOIL Moist, fertile

HARDINESS Z7–9 H9–7

FLOWERING Early spring

C

Clematis 'Bill MacKenzie'

NOTED FOR ITS MASS OF SMALL FLOWERS followed by a superb show of silvery seedheads, this clematis needs to be planted where its flowers receive full sun while its roots enjoy moist shade. Grow it on the cool side of a sturdy old tree, for example, and train the stems around to the sunny side and up into the branches. You can also let it run over a large old tree stump. Pruning is not required for aerial flowers, but for blooms closer to the base of the stems, cut them back to 8in (20cm) above the ground in early spring.

OTHER VARIETIES *C. flammula* (star-shaped, scented, white flowers); *C. tangutica* (bell-shaped, yellow flowers); *C. viticella* (bell-shaped, blue, purple, or rose red flowers with yellow centers).

PLANT PROFILE

HEIGHT 22ft (7m)

SPREAD 10ft (3m)

SITE Full sun or partial shade

SOIL Moist, fertile

HARDINESS Z6–9 H9–6

FLOWERING Midsummer to late autumn

Clematis cirrhosa 'Freckles'

C

THIS WINTER–BLOOMING, CLIMBING EVERGREEN can start flowering sporadically in late autumn, with a few flowers still showing in the spring. The flowers are creamy pink with brownish red spots and are slightly scented, while the leaves are finely cut, with a bronze tinge in the autumn. It needs a sheltered sunny site against a wall, where it can be fully appreciated. Plant it with its roots in shaded, moist, rich soil and with its head in the sun. Prune immediately after flowering, if required, to restrict its size.

OTHER VARIETY *C. montana* (very vigorous, white flowers with yellow centers).

PLANT PROFILE
HEIGHT 10ft (3m)
SPREAD 5ft (1.5m)
SITE Full sun
SOIL Moist, fertile
HARDINESS Z7–9 H9–7
FLOWERING Mid- or late winter

C | *Clematis macropetala* 'Markham's Pink'

WITH EYE-CATCHING COLORS from soft pink to rosy mauve, this Chinese deciduous climber has 4in- (10cm-) wide flowers and almost equally attractive, fluffy seedheads in the autumn. Gardener, poet, and novelist Vita Sackville-West famously grew it out of an Ali Baba jar with a blue *Clematis macropetala*. It tolerates exposed sites, but prefers to have its roots in shaded, moist, rich soil while the flowers are in the sun. After flowering, remove dead and weak stems, and cut back the others only to keep it in check.

OTHER VARIETIES *C. cirrhosa* var. *balearica* (pale cream flowers with reddish brown speckles); *C. montana* var. *rubens* (pink flowers, purple-flushed, mid-green leaves).

PLANT PROFILE

HEIGHT 10ft (3m)

SPREAD 5ft (1.5m)

SITE Full sun, partial shade

SOIL Moist, fertile

HARDINESS Z6–9 H9–3

FLOWERING Spring to early summer

Clematis montana f. *grandiflora*

C

A VIGOROUS, DECIDUOUS CLEMATIS, this is one of the best climbers for training through a tall tree or over a large wall or shed. It has a two-week flowering period when the white, 3in- (8cm-) wide flowers are an incredible sight. If it is being grown with another clematis, choose one that flowers in midsummer to carry on the show. When growing it through a tree, pruning is not necessary, but if it becomes overgrown, cut it back immediately after flowering. Water well during dry periods in summer, when it puts on new growth for the following year's flower display.

PLANT PROFILE

HEIGHT 30ft (10m)

SPREAD 12ft (4m)

SITE Full sun

SOIL Moist, fertile

HARDINESS Z6–9 H9–3

FLOWERING Late spring and early summer

C | *Clematis* 'Perle d'Azur'

FOR COVERING WALLS or growing over a pergola, this vigorous, free-flowering, azure blue deciduous clematis is perfect. You can even construct a sturdy wooden vertical frame in the border, with wires between, and allow it to climb up and produce a wall of blue. Since the 3in- (8cm-) wide flowers are on the lighter side of blue, they look darker in partial shade and paler in full sun. Prune in early spring to a strong bud 8in (20cm) above ground level.

OTHER VARIETIES *C.* 'Comtesse de Bouchaud' (large, bright mauve-pink flowers); *C.* 'Ernest Markham' (vivid magenta flowers); *C.* 'Gipsy Queen' (violet-purple flowers with red centers); *C.* 'Hagley Hybrid' (pinkish mauve flowers); *C.* 'Jackmanii' (dark purple flowers).

PLANT PROFILE
HEIGHT 10ft (3m)
SPREAD 3ft (1m)
SITE Sun or partial shade
SOIL Moist, fertile
HARDINESS Z4–9 H9–1
FLOWERING Midsummer to early autumn

Clematis 'Proteus'

C

THE FIRST BATCH OF BLOOMS from this vigorous, summer–flowering climber are up to 8in (20cm) wide, making it one of the best double-flowered, rich pink clematis for this time of year. In the second half of summer, the blooms of the equally prolific second flush are single and smaller, up to 6in (15cm) wide. The color can look rather washed out in full sun, and it should be planted in light shade, with the roots in moist, rich soil. Prune out dead and spindly stems in early spring, and cut back the rest to a healthy bud.

OTHER VARIETIES *C.* 'Beauty of Worcester' (deep blue flowers with white centers); *C.* 'Jackmanii Alba' (blue-tinged flowers with brown centers); *C.* 'Vyvyan Pennell' (lilac flowers with golden yellow centers).

PLANT PROFILE
HEIGHT 10ft (3m)
SPREAD 3ft (1m)
SITE Full sun or semi-shade
SOIL Moist, fertile
HARDINESS Z4–9 H9–1
FLOWERING Mid-to late summer

C | *Clematis rehderiana*

VIGOROUS, FREE-FLOWERING, AND DECIDUOUS, this clematis is ideal for sending up a large tree, where it will produce a creamy yellow show in the upper branches throughout the second half of summer and into autumn. During very dry spells in early summer, make sure that it is well watered to prevent stress. It needs to be planted in shaded, moist, rich soil where the flowers will receive plenty of sun. Vigorous climbers like this do not need much pruning if growing up a tree, but for flowers lower down the stems, cut back in spring to 8in (20cm) above ground level.

OTHER VARIETIES *C. flammula* (white flowers); *C. integrifolia* (blue flowers); *C. tangutica* (yellow flowers, fluffy seedheads).

PLANT PROFILE
HEIGHT 22ft (7m)
SPREAD 10ft (3m)
SITE Sun or partial shade
SOIL Moist, fertile
HARDINESS Z6–9 H9–6
FLOWERING Midsummer to late autumn

Clematis viticella 'Purpurea Plena Elegans'

C

WITH ITS PURPLE-PINK DOUBLE FLOWERS, this is one of the best viticellas, and it can be grown up through other sturdy climbers, such as roses, using them as support. Alternatively, grow it over a pergola or through a large shrub. The roots need to be in shaded, moist, rich soil while the flowers are in the sun. Prune back to 8in (20cm) above the ground in early spring, and mulch with compost in late winter after a night of rain to lock moisture in the ground. Make sure that the mulch is not in contact with the plant's stems.

OTHER VARIETIES *C.* 'Etoile Violette' (violet-purple flowers); *C.* 'Madame Julia Correvon' (wine red flowers); *C.* 'Niobe' (deep red flowers); *C.* 'Rouge Cardinal' (crimson flowers).

PLANT PROFILE
HEIGHT 10ft (3m)
SPREAD 3ft (1m)
SITE Sun or partial shade
SOIL Moist, fertile
HARDINESS Z5–9 H9–1
FLOWERING Midsummer to late autumn

Suckers growing around a shrub should be cut off where they meet the root; for new plants, remove them with a few roots intact and replant them.

C | *Clerodendrum trichotomum* Harlequin glorybower

THIS SPECTACULAR END-OF-SUMMER deciduous shrub or small tree for a woodland garden will struggle in cold winds and, as a result, grow slowly. In such conditions it could take six years to reach a height of 6ft (2m) and flower. It is vital, therefore, that you plant it in a sunny, sheltered position in free-draining soil where it will reward you in late summer with masses of small, starlike flowers with a scent similar to jasmine. The flowers are followed by eye-catching blue berries, each set in a red cup, which keep the show going well into autumn. Prune it for shape in early spring.

OTHER VARIETIES *C. bungei* (fragrant, dark pink flowers, young leaves tinged purple); *C. trichotomum* var. *fargesii* (bronze young leaves).

PLANT PROFILE

HEIGHT 20ft (6m)

SPREAD 20ft (6m)

SITE Full sun

SOIL Fertile, free-draining

HARDINESS Z7–9 H9–7

FLOWERING Late summer to midautumn

Clethra alnifolia Sweet pepper bush

C

TYPICALLY FOUND IN WOODLAND GARDENS, this deciduous, upright shrub must be grown in rich, free-draining, acidic soil in order to thrive. The leaves are 4in (10cm) long, and in summer it produces spikes of tiny white flowers with a sweet, gentle scent. Every few years, prune back some of the old wood to near ground level to clear the way for replacement stems to come through. You can also prune in late winter, removing any dead or damaged wood, to create an open network of stems.

OTHER VARIETIES *C. barbinervis* (white flowers, leaves turn red and yellow in autumn, peeling bark when mature); *C. delavayi* (white flowers from pink buds, blue-green leaves).

PLANT PROFILE
HEIGHT 8ft (2.5m)
SPREAD 8ft (2.5m)
SITE Partial or dappled shade
SOIL Acidic, fertile, free-draining
HARDINESS Z3–9 H9–1
FLOWERING Late summer and early autumn

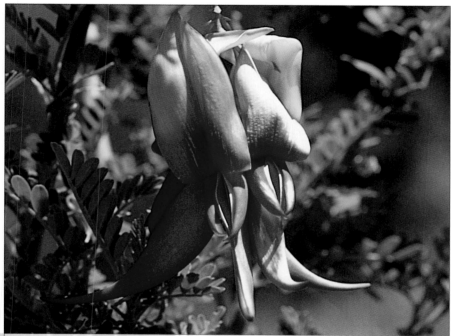

C | *Clianthus puniceus* Lobster claw

THIS IS A FUN, EVERGREEN SHRUB that features quirky, bright red flowers, thought by some to look like a lobster's claws (the plant is also sometimes commonly known as parrot's bill). It is quite fussy in its growing requirements, needing a sunny, sheltered site, preferably against a protective wall for support. Plant it in average, free-draining soil—standing in cold, wet ground throughout winter will prove lethal—and apply a thick mulch of compost in autumn to protect it. If the top growth is cut back by frost, new shoots will, in most cases, emerge from the ground the following spring.

OTHER VARIETIES *C. puniceus* 'Albus' (white flowers flushed green); *C. puniceus* 'Roseus' (dark rose pink flowers).

PLANT PROFILE
HEIGHT 12ft (4m)
SPREAD 10ft (3m)
SITE Full sun
SOIL Average, free-draining
HARDINESS Z7–11 H12–7
FLOWERING Spring to early summer

Cobaea scandens Cathedral bell

C

SPECTACULAR AND INCREDIBLY VIGOROUS, this tender climber is easily capable of sprinting up to 15ft (5m) in a single summer, when it produces fleshy, bell-shaped flowers about 2in (5cm) wide. Choose the planting site with care because once the stems take off, they will latch onto anything within reach. Give it a clear run up a sunny trellis, for example, or a fence or wall with horizontal wires firmly attached to act as supports. In hot summers, the flowers will be followed by egg-shaped, inedible, greenish fruit. Provide moist but free-draining, average soil, and grow it as an annual in cooler areas because it will not survive low temperatures.

PLANT PROFILE

HEIGHT 30–70ft (10–20m)

SITE Full sun

SOIL Moist but free-draining

HARDINESS Z11–13 H12–10

FLOWERING Summer to autumn

C

Codonopsis clematidea Bonnet bellflower

THIS FIRST-RATE, TWINING PERENNIAL climber never gets out of hand, and produces a show of beautiful bell-shaped flowers. In the spring, fragile, easily broken stems emerge from the ground, and later the round buds open to reveal nodding pale blue flowers with a blue circular ring and yellow and black markings inside. Plant it where the flowers enjoy full sun and the roots cool, moist shade. It also needs protection from damaging winds and from slugs and snails, which can quickly devour the thin stems.

OTHER VARIETIES *C. convolvulacea* (violet-blue flowers); *C. lanceolata* (mauve-flushed, greeny white flowers); *C. ovata* (greenish blue flowers).

PLANT PROFILE
HEIGHT 15ft (5m)
SITE Sun or partial shade
SOIL Moist
HARDINESS Z7–9 H9–7
FLOWERING Late summer

Colletia paradoxa Bodkin spine plant

C

THIS SOUTH AMERICAN SHRUB is both a beauty and a beast. It has pretty, almond-scented, creamy white flowers, but also produces the most lethal green spines—large, stiff, and triangular. It is a strange shrub in other respects because it hardly has any leaves. An architectural plant with a difference, it could be used as a secure "barbed-wire" barrier for your garden boundary. Plant it in a sunny, sheltered site in soil with excellent drainage. A thick winter mulch of compost is also necessary in the colder zones of its hardiness range. If you want an even bushier, spinier plant, pinch out the growing tips when they are young.

OTHER VARIETY *C. hystrix* (tubular, fragrant, white flowers).

PLANT PROFILE	
HEIGHT 10ft (3m)	
SPREAD 15ft (5m)	
SITE Full sun	
SOIL Free-draining	
HARDINESS Z7–11 H12–7	
FLOWERING Autumn	

C | *Colquhounia coccinea* Himalayan mint shrub

USUALLY EVERGREEN, EXCEPT IN COLD WINTERS, this plant has two chief assets. In addition to 8in- (20cm-) long, pointed leaves that are aromatic when crushed, it also produces bright orange to scarlet flowers on short spikes. A highly desirable shrub, it cannot be grown in an exposed garden, and to flourish it needs a sunny, sheltered position in average, free-draining soil. If the topgrowth is cut back by a light frost, new shoots should emerge from ground level the following spring. Where grown in a frost-free area during winter, you should prune it hard to the bottom framework of stems in the spring to stimulate fresh, new growth.

PLANT PROFILE
HEIGHT 8ft (2.5m)
SPREAD 8ft (2.5m)
SITE Full sun
SOIL Average, free-draining
HARDINESS Z8–9 H9–8
FLOWERING Late summer

Colutea arborescens Bladder senna

C

THE COMMON NAME of this deciduous shrub describes the unusual shape of its large seed pods, which look like bladders or kidney beans when seen from a distance. The pods ping open in autumn, flinging out the seed in all directions. During the summer it is bushy and quite eye-catching, with clusters of ¾in- (2cm-) long yellow flowers and attractive, divided, pale green leaves. It will grow well in average, free-draining soil, and should be pruned in early spring, when you can cut it back to maintain its shape.

OTHER VARIETY *C. x media* (orange-brown flowers, greenish brown pods); *C. orientalis* (smaller-growing, copper-red flowers, bluish green leaves, pale brown pods).

PLANT PROFILE	
HEIGHT 10ft (3m)	
SPREAD 10ft (3m)	
SITE Full sun	
SOIL Average, free-draining	
HARDINESS Z6–8 H8–6	
FLOWERING Summer	

C | *Convolvulus cneorum* Silverbush

FOR A GAP AT THE FRONT OF A BORDER, this is an excellent choice of evergreen shrub. It will flower, from pink buds, throughout the summer, with open, trumpet-shaped, yellow-centered white blooms standing out well against the silky, silver-green leaves. The flowers also contrast well with crimson and blue blooms. The oval-shaped plants perform best in moderately fertile or even poor soil, and they also require good drainage and wall-to-wall sun. In areas with heavy, cold, wet winter soil, it is best to plant them in containers of gritty soil mix that can be positioned in a sheltered spot over winter.

OTHER VARIETY *C. sabatius* (pale to deep lavender-blue flowers).

PLANT PROFILE
HEIGHT 24in (60cm)
SPREAD 3ft (1m)
SITE Full sun
SOIL Free-draining
HARDINESS Z8–11 H12–8
FLOWERING Late spring to summer

Cornus alba 'Sibirica' Red-barked dogwood

THIS SUPERB DECIDUOUS SHRUB offers one of the best shows in the winter garden. It has striking, bright red, new stems that sprout out of the ground like the spines of a giant porcupine and retain their color for a year or two. Prune every spring, or every other year, to just above ground level to force up new colored growth (at the expense of any flowers). In large gardens, these dogwoods are best planted in groups. 'Sibirica' tolerates a wide range of soils, including heavy clay. For blazing stems, grow it in full sun.

OTHER VARIETIES *C. alba* 'Aurea' (yellow leaves, red stems); *C. alba* 'Elegantissima' (variegated foliage, red stems); *C. alba* 'Kesselringii' (blackish purple winter shoots, red and purple leaves in autumn).

PLANT PROFILE
HEIGHT 8ft (2.5m)
SPREAD 8ft (2.5m)
SITE Full sun
SOIL Fertile, free-draining
HARDINESS Z2–8 H8–1
FLOWERING Late spring and early summer

C | *Cornus mas* Cornelian cherry

WITH CLUSTERS OF SMALL YELLOW FLOWERS that appear before the leaves, this shrub is a bright choice for a winter garden. The foliage flares up reddish purple in the autumn before falling, when bright red berries also form. It thrives in most soils, except extremes of wet and dry, and pruning in early summer is necessary only to keep it in shape. A smaller choice for medium-size gardens is the 6ft– (2m–) high *Cornus mas* 'Aureoelegantissima', the leaves of which are edged with yellow and pink.

OTHER VARIETIES *C.* 'Ormonde' (purple and green flowers with pink-tipped white bracts, leaves turn orange, red, or purple in autumn); *C. sanguinea* 'Winter Beauty' (orange-yellow and red winter shoots).

PLANT PROFILE
HEIGHT 15ft (5m)
SPREAD 15ft (5m)
SITE Sun or partial shade
SOIL Moist but free-draining
HARDINESS Z5–8 H8–5
FLOWERING Late winter

Corokia cotoneaster Wire-netting bush

THE HIGHLY APPROPRIATE COMMON NAME of this evergreen shrub comes from its stiff, wiry, tangled net of stems. Its curious, tiny leaves are spoon-shaped, and the small yellow flowers are gently scented and followed by bright red berries. None of the corokias is very hardy, but *Corokia cotoneaster* is one of the toughest. Despite this, it still needs a sunny, sheltered position with free-draining, rich soil. A little gentle pruning may be necessary after flowering to maintain its shape, but it will tolerate harder pruning if required.

OTHER VARIETIES *C. x virgata* (fragrant yellow flowers followed by yellow or orange fruit); *C. x virgata* 'Bronze King' (dark bronze-tinged foliage); *C. x virgata* 'Yellow Wonder' (golden yellow fruit).

PLANT PROFILE	
HEIGHT 8ft (2.5m)	
SPREAD 8ft (2.5m)	
SITE Full sun	
SOIL Fertile, free-draining	
HARDINESS Z9–11 H12–10	
FLOWERING Late spring	

C   *Coronilla valentina* subsp. *glauca* 'Variegata' Crown vetch

GIVEN THE RIGHT CONDITIONS, this extremely bushy, fruity-scented evergreen with cream-margined leaves will flower prolifically—not just once, from late winter to early spring, but again in late summer. It requires a sunny position, shelter from cold winter winds, and free-draining, average soil. The base of a south-facing wall is an ideal location; or, without the right conditions, grow it in a conservatory. Pruning is not necessary, but if it becomes straggly and needs neatening up, cut it back in midspring and it will quickly reshoot.

OTHER VARIETIES *C. valentina* subsp. *glauca* (smaller-growing, blue-green leaves); *C. valentina* subsp. *glauca* 'Citrina' (pale yellow flowers).

PLANT PROFILE

HEIGHT 5ft (1.5m)

SPREAD 5ft (1.5m)

SITE Full sun

SOIL Average, free-draining

HARDINESS Z8–9

FLOWERING Late winter, early spring and summer

Correa backhouseana Australian fuchsia

THE GOOD NEWS is that this native of southern Australia is capable of flowering all through the winter, but the bad news is that it needs a very sheltered, warm spot. The base of a sunny, protective wall is ideal as long as the soil is moist, rich, and even slightly acidic. If outdoor conditions are not right, you can grow it in a border or large container in a conservatory or heated greenhouse, where it should reliably produce 1in- (2.5cm-) long tubular, reddish green or cream flowers, on a dense network of hairy, rust red twigs.

OTHER VARIETIES *C.* 'Dusky Bells' (smaller-growing, dusky carmine-red flowers); *C.* 'Mannii' (red flowers); *C. reflexa* (green, white, pink, or red flowers, sometimes with green or cream petal tips).

PLANT PROFILE	
HEIGHT	3–6ft (1–2m)
SPREAD	5–8ft (1.5–2.5m)
SITE	Full sun
SOIL	Moist, fertile
HARDINESS	Z9–10 H10–8
FLOWERING	Late autumn to late spring

C | *Corylopsis pauciflora* Buttercup winter hazel

AS ONE OF THE BEST SHRUBS for acidic soil and light shade, *Corylopsis pauciflora* makes a thicketlike mass of twiggy growth that is covered in pale yellow flowers in the second half of spring. The blooms have a faint scent that is only detectable when you get up close. It is almost maintenance-free, and pruning is unnecessary—not to mention nearly impossible, given its dense growth—but you can remove dead or damaged wood at any time of year. Good alternatives include the lemon yellow *C. sinensis* var. *sinensis*.

OTHER VARIETIES *C. glabrescens* (taller-growing, hanging clusters of pale yellow flowers, dark green leaves, blue-green beneath); *C. sinensis* var. *sinensis* 'Spring Purple' (dark plum purple young leaves).

PLANT PROFILE
HEIGHT 5ft (1.5m)
SPREAD 5ft (1.5m)
SITE Partial shade
SOIL Acidic, fertile, moist but free-draining
HARDINESS Z3–9 H9–1
FLOWERING Late spring

Corylus avellana 'Contorta' Corkscrew hazel

C

WITH TWISTY, CORKSCREWLIKE bare branches, this deciduous shrub is a good choice for the winter garden. The branches make a lively architectural shape when viewed against the sky, and they are even more eye-catching at the end of winter when pale yellow, dangling catkins appear; these are well worth including as part of an indoor arrangement. Most soils are fine, as long as they are free-draining and fertile. Pruning is not necessary, but remove any straight stems and prune to thin it out or for size in late winter.

OTHER VARIETIES *C. avellana* (broadly heart-shaped, round-tipped leaves, yellow catkins); *C. avellana* 'Aurea' (bright yellow young leaves).

PLANT PROFILE
HEIGHT 15ft (5m)
SPREAD 15ft (5m)
SITE Full sun or semishade
SOIL Fertile, free-draining
HARDINESS Z3–9 H9–1
FLOWERING Late winter and early spring

C | *Corylus maxima* 'Purpurea' Filbert

THIS IS AN EXCELLENT HAZEL to grow for its edible autumn nuts, late-winter purple-tinged catkins, and young, rich purple spring foliage, which gradually darkens throughout the summer. 'Purpurea' does not have the unusual branches of the corkscrew hazel (*Corylus avellana* 'Contorta'), but it does grow a little taller, and is equally unfussy about its growing conditions, needing soil with very good drainage more than anything else. Its purple-tinged catkins also make a beautiful contribution to cut-flower arrangements.

OTHER VARIETIES *C. avellana* (yellow catkins in late winter); *C. avellana* 'Aurea' (bright yellow young leaves).

PLANT PROFILE
HEIGHT 20ft (6m)
SPREAD 15ft (5m)
SITE Full sun or partial shade
SOIL Free-draining
HARDINESS Z4–9 H9–1
FLOWERING Late winter

Cotinus coggygria Smoke bush

C

INJECTING INTEREST INTO AN AUTUMN BORDER, the leaves of this bushy deciduous shrub turn arresting shades of red and yellow before they fall. Its common name describes the tiny flowers on its mature stems, which produce a blurred, smoky effect throughout the summer. For the best flowers and leaf color, it needs average soil that is neither too moist nor overly rich, and a long hot summer. It is a first-rate plant but does require space, although it can be pruned in early spring to restrict its size and remove dead wood.

OTHER VARIETIES *C. coggygria* 'Notcutt's Variety' (wine red leaves, purple-pink flowers); *C. coggygria* 'Royal Purple' (dark purple foliage); *C.* 'Flame' (orange-red autumn tints); *C.* 'Grace' (bright red autumn tints).

PLANT PROFILE

HEIGHT 15ft (5m)

SPREAD 15ft (5m)

SITE Full sun or partial shade

SOIL Average, free-draining

HARDINESS Z5–9 H9–3

FLOWERING Summer

C

Cotoneaster horizontalis

THE BEST REASON for growing this plant is its fishbonelike stems, which are covered with scarlet berries in autumn and into winter, if the birds leave them alone. Other attractions include deciduous red autumn leaves, white pink-tinged flowers in the spring, and its ability to grow on shady walls. Like all cotoneasters, it tolerates most soils, but avoid soaking-wet ground and overfertilizing. Prune in late winter to accentuate its shape.

OTHER VARIETIES *C. adpressus* (shorter-growing, red-tinged white flowers, bright red fruit); *C. conspicuus* (evergreen, white flowers, red fruit); *C.* 'Hybridus Pendulus' (taller-growing, white flowers, red fruit); *C. procumbens* (green leaves, purplish when young).

PLANT PROFILE
HEIGHT 3ft (1m)
SPREAD 5ft (1.5m)
SITE Full sun, but shade-tolerant
SOIL Average, free-draining
HARDINESS Z4–7 H7–3
FLOWERING Late spring

Cotoneaster 'Rothschildianus'

THE ARCHING STEMS of this semievergreen to evergreen shrub are covered in long, thin, pale green leaves. There is a good show of whitish flowers at the start of summer, followed by butter yellow berries that hang on into winter. An excellent partner for a red-berried cotoneaster in a shrub border, you can also grow it as a hedge or at the edge of a wooded area of the garden. Like all cotoneasters, it tolerates most soils, but avoid soaking-wet or very fertile ground.

OTHER VARIETIES *C. franchettii* (smaller-growing, red-flushed white flowers, orange-red fruit); *C. lacteus* (green leaves, white-felted beneath, milky white flowers, red fruit); *C. salicifolius* (white flowers, red fruit).

PLANT PROFILE	
HEIGHT	15ft (5m)
SPREAD	15ft (5m)
SITE	Sun or partial shade
SOIL	Average, free-draining
HARDINESS	Z6–8 H8–6
FLOWERING	Early summer

C | *Crinodendron hookerianum* Lantern tree

TYPICALLY A LARGE EVERGREEN SHRUB, or possibly a small tree in the right conditions, this Chilean plant has downward-pointing flowers that look like miniature lanterns or tulips. Although flower buds appear in the autumn, they do not begin to fatten until the spring, opening right at the end of that season. The lantern tree is slightly fussy, needing a sheltered site to avoid leaf scorch, and the roots must be in cool, moist, shaded, acidic soil. When provided with these conditions, it will reward you with an impressive show. Any pruning necessary to maintain shape should be done after flowering.

OTHER VARIETY *C. patagua* (scented, white fringed flowers).

PLANT PROFILE
HEIGHT 12ft (4m) after 12 years
SPREAD 8ft (2.5m) after 12 years
SITE Full sun to partial shade
SOIL Acidic, moist
HARDINESS Z9–11 H12–9
FLOWERING All summer

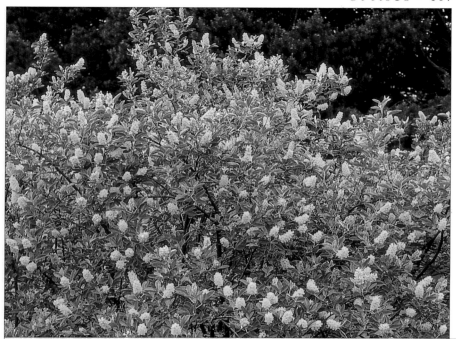

Cytisus battandieri Pineapple broom

C

THE BRIGHT YELLOW FLOWERS of this deciduous, treelike shrub are up to 6in (15cm) long and smell of freshly cut pineapples, which accounts for its common name. The silvery leaves can be 4in (10cm) long. It generally thrives best against a sunny, sheltered wall, although you can grow it in a protected border. It dislikes being moved once it is in the ground, and requires free-draining, poor, acidic soil—wet, heavy ground will prove fatal.

OTHER VARIETIES *C.* 'Burkwoodii' (dark pink flowers with yellow margins); *C.* x *kewensis* (cream flowers); *C. multiflorus* (white flowers); *C.* 'Zeelandia' (creamy white and lilac-pink flowers).

PLANT PROFILE
HEIGHT 15ft (5m)
SPREAD 15ft (5m)
SITE Full sun
SOIL Acidic, poor, free-draining
HARDINESS Z7–9 H9–7
FLOWERING Mid- and late summer

C | *Cytisus x praecox* 'Allgold' Broom

ONE OF THE PARENTS of this attractive broom is dense and bushy, while the other is incredibly free-flowering: put them together and they produce this deciduous, compact shrub, which has long-lasting, dark yellow flowers. It is easy to grow, needing average garden soil, which can be poor and acidic. Prune it after flowering for shape, if necessary, but don't cut back into the old wood—the less 'Allgold' is pruned, the better the flowering will be.

OTHER VARIETIES *C.* 'Boskoop Ruby' (red flowers); *C.* 'Hollandia' (cream and dark pink flowers); *C.* 'Lena' (dark yellow flowers with bright red wings).

PLANT PROFILE
HEIGHT 4ft (1.2m)
SPREAD 5ft (1.5m)
SITE Full sun
SOIL Average
HARDINESS Z6–9 H9–1
FLOWERING Mid- and late spring

Daboecia cantabrica subsp. *scotica* 'William Buchanan' **Heather**

 D

THIS DWARF SHRUB is suitable for acidic soil and is a good choice for the front of a border, since it flowers reliably throughout the growing season. It can also be grown in rock gardens or raised beds, and needs to be in a sheltered position. The brightly colored flowers are borne well clear of the evergreen leaves. The pruning regimen could not be simpler—a light, all-over trim in the spring to remove last year's dead flower stalks, thus keeping the plant neat and smart. If you grow two or three different kinds together, you can create a patchwork quilt of colors.

OTHER VARIETIES *D. cantabrica* 'Bicolor' (flowers in white, pink and beet red); *D. cantabrica* subsp. *scotica* 'Silverwells' (white flowers).

PLANT PROFILE
HEIGHT 14in (35cm)
SPREAD 22in (55cm)
SITE Full sun
SOIL Free-draining
HARDINESS Z6–8 H8–6
FLOWERING Late spring to midautumn

D

Danae racemosa Alexandrian laurel

A BIT OF A BOTANICAL CURIOSITY, the leaves of this unusual, compact, slow-growing evergreen shrub from woodland regions in Turkey are, in fact, flat branches. At the start of the summer, small, greenish yellow flowers appear, and these are followed by tiny, glossy red or orange-red berries that make more impact than the blooms. Both the unusual branches and the bright berries are suitable for a cut-flower display. For the best results, grow Alexandrian laurel in rich, moist but free-draining soil, and choose a position where it has shelter from strong, damaging winds. Cut old stems back hard in the spring, before the new season's growth gets under way.

PLANT PROFILE
HEIGHT 3ft (1m)
SPREAD 3ft (1m)
SITE Sun or shade
SOIL Fertile, moist but free-draining
HARDINESS Z6–9 H9–2
FLOWERING Early summer

Daphne mezereum February daphne

D

THE FABULOUS SCENT from tiny flowers at the top of bare stems in late winter and early spring is the main attraction. In exposed and cold areas, provide a sunny, sheltered spot where the scent will linger. It thrives on alkaline soil but is quite happy on many different soils, provided they are moist but free-draining and reasonably fertile—the roots must not dry out or become waterlogged. Don't be put off by its reputation for being tricky to grow, but do note that the sap can be an irritant and that all parts are toxic if eaten.

OTHER VARIETIES *D. bholua* var. *glacialis* 'Gurkha' (white flowers flushed purple-pink, blackish purple fruit); *D. cneorum* 'Eximia' (shorter-growing, rose pink flowers from crimson buds).

PLANT PROFILE
HEIGHT 4ft (1.2m)
SPREAD 3ft (1m)
SITE Full sun or light shade
SOIL Moist but free-draining
HARDINESS Z5–8 H8–5
FLOWERING Late winter and early spring

D | *Decaisnea fargesii* Blue bean bush

THIS DECIDUOUS, UPRIGHT CHINESE SHRUB has three quirky features that make it very popular. First, after flowering it produces 4in- (10cm-) long seed pods that look like metallic blue broad beans. Second, the drooping, bell-shaped, green or yellow-green early-summer flowers do not actually have any petals. Third, the leaves are up to 1m (3ft) long and consist of up to 25 leaflets that turn an attractive yellow in the autumn. It is easy to grow, given the right conditions—rich, moist but free-draining soil, and shelter from strong winds. A position in a wooded area of the garden provides the necessary shelter.

PLANT PROFILE
HEIGHT 20ft (6m)
SPREAD 20ft (6m)
SITE Sun or partial shade
SOIL Fertile, moist but free-draining
HARDINESS Z7–9 H9–7
FLOWERING Early summer

Dendromecon rigida Tree poppy

IN ITS NATIVE CALIFORNIA, the tree poppy grows in full sun on dry, rocky slopes, which is why it needs a warm, sheltered spot to thrive in the garden. Choose a planting position with free-draining soil—perhaps in a gravel garden, on top of a bank, or at the foot of a wall—where it will produce blue-green, willowlike leaves, and bright yellow, poppylike, gently scented flowers. When it is being wall-trained, cut back the flowered stems in summer after flowering to just 2–4 buds from the main framework. If growing it as a bush, in early spring cut back winter-damaged or weak stems to a healthy, outward-facing bud. It can be grown close to *Fremontodendron* 'California Glory', which enjoys the same conditions.

PLANT PROFILE
HEIGHT 10ft (3m)
SPREAD 10ft (3m)
SITE Full sun
SOIL Free-draining
HARDINESS Z9–11 H12–9
FLOWERING Spring to autumn

D | *Desfontainia spinosa*

FOR GARDENS WITH ACIDIC OR NEUTRAL SOIL, this dramatic South American plant is ideal. It produces showy, red, tubular flowers with yellow tips and makes a medium-sized, slow-growing evergreen bush with shiny, hollylike leaves. You can prolong the flowering period by keeping the soil moist with a thick mulch of compost, which should be applied in the spring after a downpour. It needs a protected, sheltered site—for example, at the foot of a wall where it will receive shade in the middle of the day. Pruning is rarely needed, but you can give it a light trim in spring for shape. If it is not looking happy in its position, keep trying it in different places because, when it does thrive, it is a marvelous shrub.

PLANT PROFILE

HEIGHT 6ft (2m)

SPREAD 6ft (2m)

SITE Dappled shade

SOIL Moist

HARDINESS Z8–11 H12–8

FLOWERING Midsummer to late autumn

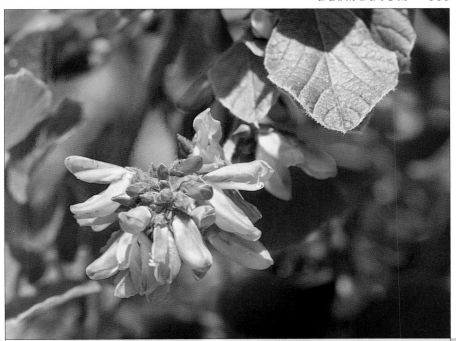

Desmodium elegans

D

THIS SUBTLE, UNASSUMING SHRUB really comes into its own at the end of the growing season, when many other garden plants are beginning to look a little tired and past their best. The large, 10in- (25cm-) long leaves consist of three leaflets, and they are joined by airy sprays, about 8in (20cm) long, of tiny lilac to deep pink flowers. The stems should be cut back in the spring in order to force up strong, new growth. *Desmodium elegans* requires free-draining soil and a warm, sheltered position to thrive.

OTHER VARIETY *D. yunnanense* (taller-growing, clusters of pealike, purple flowers, pale green downy leaves).

PLANT PROFILE	
HEIGHT 5ft (1.5m)	
SPREAD 5ft (1.5m)	
SITE Full sun	
SOIL Free-draining	
HARDINESS Z8–11 H12–8	
FLOWERING Late summer to autumn	

D *Deutzia* x *hybrida* 'Mont Rose'

ERECT, DENSE AND VIGOROUS, this is a medium-high, deciduous shrub with arching stems of five-petaled, purple-pink blooms set against dark green foliage. A beautiful plant for a border, it is also extremely easy to grow and will tolerate most soils, but don't let the ground dry out in the summer. To avoid this, add a thick mulch of compost around the plant, avoiding the stems, in the spring after a night of heavy rain to help lock moisture in the ground. There are also many excellent spring- and summer-flowering alternatives.

OTHER VARIETIES *D. compacta* 'Lavender Time' (taller-growing, lilac flowers fading with age); *D.* x *kalmiiflora* (taller-growing, star-shaped, deep pink flowers).

PLANT PROFILE
HEIGHT 4ft (1.2m)
SPREAD 4ft (1.2m)
SITE Full sun or light shade
SOIL Moist but free-draining
HARDINESS Z5–8 H8–6
FLOWERING Early summer

Dipelta floribunda

SWEETLY SCENTED, TUBULAR FLOWERS, opening at the end of spring, make this substantial deciduous shrub a real garden asset. It is multistemmed and open-looking, with thin, peeling bark and beautiful, 4in- (10cm-) long, pointed leaves. It grows in rich, free-draining soil, and will flourish in chalky, alkaline conditions. After the pale pink flowers are finished blooming, prune the flowered stems back to strong buds. You can remove one-fourth of the old stems of established plants back to the base every few years to encourage new growth, and to keep an open framework of branches.

OTHER VARIETY *D. yunnanensis* (smaller-growing, white flowers with orange markings).

PLANT PROFILE	
HEIGHT 12ft (4m)	
SPREAD 12ft (4m)	
SITE Sun or partial shade	
SOIL Fertile, free-draining	
HARDINESS Z6–9 H9–6	
FLOWERING Late spring and early summer	

D | *Disanthus cercidifolius*

FOUND GROWING IN WOODLAND AND MOUNTAINOUS regions of China and Japan, this decorative deciduous shrub is highly rated for the autumn garden. Its blue-green leaves turn flamboyant shades of red, orange, and purple at the end of the year, with all colors on display at the same time. In addition, you have the bonus of faintly scented, spidery, rose red flowers that also appear in autumn. Given its modest size, and that it can be grown as a showy boundary plant, it deserves to be far more popular than it is. Make sure you provide it with a sheltered position where it will be protected from destructive strong winds.

PLANT PROFILE
HEIGHT 10ft (3m)
SPREAD 10ft (3m)
SITE Full sun
SOIL Moist, free-draining
HARDINESS Z5–8 H8–5
FLOWERING Midautumn

Dodonaea viscosa 'Purpurea' Hop bush

D

THE FLOWERS ON THIS SPREADING, evergreen, Australian shrub or small tree are quite insignificant, but the winged seed capsules in the summer and autumn put on a far better show, and come in shades ranging from pink to reddish brown, light brown, purple, and yellow. The leaves are equally attractive, with a strong purplish red hue. Young plants, especially if you are growing them as a temporary hedge, should have their growing tips pinched out to make them bushier and to give a better show of colored foliage. Grow the hop bush in moist but free-draining soil in a protected, sunny spot in summer, but bring it indoors in late autumn in colder areas.

PLANT PROFILE
HEIGHT 3–15ft (1–5m)
SPREAD 3–10ft (1–3m)
SITE Full sun
SOIL Moist, fertile, free-draining
HARDINESS Z12–15 H12–10
FLOWERING Early summer

D **|** *Dregea sinensis* Hardy hoya

THIS DECIDUOUS, SCENTED, TWINING Chinese climber is usually grown in conservatories, but it can easily be grown outside if you are prepared to pamper it a little. It needs the protection of a hot, sunny wall (with horizontal wires for it to climb up), shelter from the wind, and free-draining soil. It could also be grown over an arch outside a front or back door. The leaves are small and heart-shaped, while the clusters of tiny pink flowers that open in summer are gently scented—the perfume is more intense in a warm, windless position. Grow this climber in free-draining soil and, if space is limited, prune it in spring. Provide a protective mulch of compost over the soil, leaving the stem area clear, in the autumn.

PLANT PROFILE	
HEIGHT	10ft (3m)
SITE	Sun or partial shade
SOIL	Free-draining
HARDINESS	Z8–10 H10–8
FLOWERING	Summer

Drimys lanceolata Mountain pepper

D

UPRIGHT AND EVERGREEN, this shrub peaks in spring, when scores of small, white flowers open. If you have separate male and female shrubs, these flowers will be followed by small, dark red or black berries. Mountain pepper also has reddish young stems and shiny, scented leaves. An Australian native, it requires a degree of protection from wind and frost over the winter, and the soil should be fertile, and moist but free-draining. Pruning is rarely necessary, but unwanted or wayward stems can be removed after flowering.

OTHER VARIETY *D. winteri* (taller-growing, aromatic bark, large clusters of fragrant, ivory white flowers).

PLANT PROFILE	
HEIGHT 12ft (4m)	
SPREAD 8ft (2.5m)	
SITE Sun or partial shade	
SOIL Fertile, moist but free-draining	
HARDINESS Z9–10	
FLOWERING Mid- and late spring	

E

Eccremocarpus scaber Chilean glory flower

THIS SPECTACULAR EVERGREEN climber from South America has small, bright, brash tubular flowers. It will survive colder climates for a few years if provided with a sunny, sheltered position, but you will eventually have to replace it. It can also be grown from seed and will shoot up 8ft (2.5m) or more and flower in its first summer. If caught by a frost, the stems die, but new growth should appear in the following spring if given a winter mulch of compost. The soil should be on the light side, free-draining, and fertile. It can be pruned in spring if it has grown too large.

OTHER VARIETY *E. scaber carmineus* (carmine red flowers).

PLANT PROFILE

HEIGHT To 15ft (5m)

SITE Full sun

SOIL Fertile, free-draining

HARDINESS Z11–15 H12–10

FLOWERING Late spring to autumn

Elaeagnus x *ebbingei* 'Gilt Edge' Oleaster

E

DARK GREEN LEAVES with eye-catching yellow margins are this fast-growing evergreen's most striking feature. It makes a good backdrop for a mixed or shrub border, or you could grow it as hedging or a windbreak in a coastal garden. The more sun it gets, the better the display of autumn flowers, which, although insignificant to look at, produce a wonderful, fruity scent. Grow it in free-draining, fertile soil, and prune in the spring to keep it shapely. Remove any all-green shoots to stop the plant from eventually losing its variegation.

OTHER VARIETIES *E. angustifolia* (red-tinted branches, flowers followed by silvery yellow fruit); *E.* x *ebbingei* 'Limelight' (silvery young leaves becoming marked with pale green and yellow).

PLANT PROFILE	
HEIGHT 12ft (4m)	
SPREAD 12ft (4m)	
SITE Full sun	
SOIL Fertile, free-draining	
HARDINESS Z7–10 H10–7	
FLOWERING Autumn	

E

Elaeagnus 'Quicksilver' Oleaster

HIGHLY RATED FOR ITS SILVER-GRAY FOLIAGE, which is particularly bright in the spring, 'Quicksilver' is a fast-growing, open, deciduous shrub. The star-shaped yellow flowers open from silver buds in the summer. It can be grown as an individual focal point or as a lively foil for a wide range of other colors, from dark green to red, in a border or gravel garden. It will also grow quite happily in a windy coastal garden. Plant it in free-draining, fertile, nonalkaline soil, and prune lightly in the spring to keep it neat and shapely.

OTHER VARIETIES *E. commutata* (red-brown shoots, leaves covered with silvery scales); *E. pungens* 'Maculata' (leaf centers boldly marked with dark yellow).

PLANT PROFILE	
HEIGHT 12ft (4m)	
SPREAD 12ft (4m)	
SITE Full sun	
SOIL Fertile, free-draining	
HARDINESS Z3–8 H8–1	
FLOWERING Summer	

Eleutherococcus sieboldianus Five-leafed aralia

E

THIS TALL-GROWING DECIDUOUS SHRUB can be grown as part of a garden perimeter due to its spiny, canelike stems, which make good hedging material. It has large, hand-shaped leaves consisting of smaller leaflets, and small, star-shaped, greenish white flowers that appear from late spring. These are followed by tiny black berries. It thrives in poor, dry, free-draining soil. Don't try growing this shrub on heavy clay soil that stays wet in winter because these conditions will quickly kill it.

OTHER VARIETY *E. sieboldianus* 'Variegatus' (leaves margined with creamy white).

PLANT PROFILE
HEIGHT 8ft (2.5m)
SPREAD 8ft (2.5m)
SITE Full sun
SOIL Dry, free-draining
HARDINESS Z4–8 H9–3
FLOWERING Late spring and early summer

E

Elsholtzia stauntonii Mint shrub

THIS AUTUMN-FLOWERING, deciduous shrub is well worth growing
to add a touch of late-season color. Its tiny purple-pink flowers
are held on 6in- (15cm-) long candlelike spikes, while the equally
long leaves give off a distinct smell of mint when torn, and turn
red in the autumn before falling. It needs a sunny, sheltered position
in the garden, with rich, free-draining soil. In colder regions, grow
it in a pot and bring it under cover for the winter. In spring, cut
back all growth to the permanent framework of stems to force up
new flowering wood.

OTHER VARIETY *E. stauntonii* 'Alba' (white flowers).

PLANT PROFILE

HEIGHT 5ft (1.5m)

SPREAD 5ft (1.5m)

SITE Full sun

SOIL Fertile, free-draining

HARDINESS Z5–8 H8–5

FLOWERING Late summer
to autumn

Embothrium coccineum Chilean fire bush

E

GETTING THE SUMMER OFF to a lively start, this plant is a contender for any hot color scheme. It produces a show of abundant flower clusters, and the scarlet (occasionally yellow) tubular blooms really stand out against a background of green, glossy leaves. Chilean fire bush has the added advantages of being quick-growing, evergreen (or semievergreen, depending on climate), and multibranched. Plant it in rich, moist but free-draining soil, which can be on the acidic side, with some protection from the damaging effects of the wind.

OTHER VARIETY *E. coccineum* Lanceolatum Group 'Norquinco' (attractive narrow lance-shaped leaves).

PLANT PROFILE
HEIGHT 30ft (10m)
SPREAD 15ft (5m)
SITE Full sun or partial shade
SOIL Moist, fertile, free-draining
HARDINESS Z8–11 H12–8
FLOWERING Late spring and early summer

E *Enkianthus campanulatus*

IF YOU HAVE ACIDIC SOIL, and space to spare, try this Japanese shrub, which has heavy clusters of bell-like flowers with pink to red veining. The leaves add extra color to the autumn garden with a show of orange-yellow, turning red, before falling. Either grow one as a feature plant where its rich autumn colors can be readily seen, or combine it with other late-season performers. It requires plenty of space and a site in full sun or partial shade, although growth is not as vigorous in shadier positions.

OTHER VARIETIES *E. cernuus* f. *rubens* (rich red flowers, leaves dark red-purple in autumn); *E. chinensis* (creamy yellow flowers, leaves orange and red in autumn); *E. perulatus* (compact, smaller-growing).

PLANT PROFILE

HEIGHT 12–15ft (4–5m)

SPREAD 12–15ft (4–5m)

SITE Full sun or partial shade

SOIL Acidic, moist but free-draining

HARDINESS Z4–7 H7–3

FLOWERING Late spring and early summer

Erica arborea var. *alpina* Tree heath

LIBERALLY COVERED IN DENSE CLUSTERS of white spring flowers, you can grow this excellent plant beside other tree heaths with blooms or leaves in contrasting shades. Unlike many ericas that are ground-hugging, spreading shrubs, this is a tall, upright plant. Ideally, you should grow it in acidic, free-draining soil with well-rotted organic matter dug in before planting. Prune after it has flowered in its first two or three years, cutting back stems by two-thirds, which will encourage bushier growth. In subsequent years, prune only to keep it neat and to cut out dead and diseased wood.

OTHER VARIETIES *E. arborea* 'Albert's Gold' (gold leaves); *E. carnea* 'Ann Sparkes' (pink flowers, gold leaves).

PLANT PROFILE	
HEIGHT 6ft (2m)	
SPREAD 35in (85cm)	
SITE Full sun	
SOIL Acidic, free-draining	
HARDINESS Z9–10 H10–9	
FLOWERING Spring	

E

Erica carnea 'Foxhollow' Winter heath

MOST WINTER HEATHS have white, pink, purple, or red flowers, and this pale pink type stands out because its yellow leaves turn orange-red when the temperatures drop. Choose carefully and you can have ericas in flower from midwinter to late spring, creating a carpet of color when it is badly needed. In spring and summer, the spreading stems of evergreen leaves also block out the light and suppress weed growth. Winter heaths need acidic, free-draining soil, and should be pruned after flowering, leaving 1in (2.5cm) of topgrowth.

OTHER VARIETIES   *E. carnea* 'Adrienne Duncan' (bronze foliage); *E. carnea* 'Challenger' (bold magenta flowers); *E. carnea* 'Golden Starlet' (white flowers, lime green leaves).

PLANT PROFILE		
HEIGHT 6in (15cm)		
SPREAD 16in (40cm)		
SITE Full sun		
SOIL Free-draining		
HARDINESS Z5–7 H7–5		
FLOWERING Late winter and early spring		

Erythrina crista-galli Cock's comb

THIS WOODY-STEMMED SOUTH AMERICAN plant produces bizarre, rich red flowers toward the end of summer. These appear on stems protected by long, fierce-looking spines, which means it must be kept out of reach of children and away from paths. If you can provide a sunny, sheltered position in your garden—for example, against a warm wall—with rich, moist but free-draining soil, it should succeed. Add a protective winter mulch of compost to be safe. Cock's comb is definitely worth trying, not least for its glossy, leathery leaves, and if the topgrowth is cut back after a cold winter, new shoots should emerge at ground level the following spring. It can also be grown in a large tub, and this allows you to bring it into a conservatory over winter and take it outdoors once more for the summer season.

PLANT PROFILE
HEIGHT 8ft (2.5m)
SPREAD 5ft (1.5m)
SITE Full sun
SOIL Moist, fertile, free-draining
HARDINESS Z11–15 H12–8
FLOWERING Late summer to autumn

E | *Escallonia* 'Apple Blossom'

THESE EXCELLENT, ALL-PURPOSE SHRUBS flower from the start of summer until the autumn, and when the weather is warm, the shiny evergreen leaves also produce a gentle, sweet scent. Even better, this pretty plant tolerates coastal conditions and can be used for hedging or a windbreak. Inland, however, it needs a more sheltered site that provides protection against frost and icy winds. Escallonias thrive in well-drained soil, and if pruning is required to maintain their shape, do this immediately after flowering. In coastal gardens they may exceed 8ft (2.5m) in height and spread.

OTHER VARIETIES *E.* 'Donard Radiance' (rich pink flowers); *E.* 'Iveyi' (white flowers); *E. rubra* 'Crimson Spire' (crimson flowers).

PLANT PROFILE
HEIGHT 8ft (2.5m)
SPREAD 8ft (2.5m)
SITE Full sun
SOIL Free-draining
HARDINESS Z8–9 H9–8
FLOWERING Early and midsummer

HARD PRUNING

Pruning gum trees hard each year will restrict their size, and encourages more new, young stems with bright foliage to grow. In late spring, prune the previous year's stems back to within 2–3in (5–8cm) of the main trunk.

Eucalyptus pauciflora subsp. *niphophila* Snow gum

E

WITH WHITE BARK peeling off from midspring to autumn to reveal green, brownish red and gray bark beneath, the snow gum is a beautiful garden plant. Although officially a tree, reaching up to 20ft (6m) in height, the snow gum can be pruned hard to keep it multistemmed and shrubby, and only about 10ft (3m) high. Start this pollarding process when the plant is three years old by cutting off the stems to a low framework in late spring. This encourages new growth and the attractive immature foliage, but as a result you may not get the full effect of the peeling bark.

OTHER VARIETIES *E. gregsoniana* (white flowers, bluish green young leaves); *E. nicholii* (reddish brown bark, blue-green young leaves).

PLANT PROFILE

HEIGHT 10ft (3m)

SPREAD 10ft (3m)

SITE Full sun

SOIL Free-draining

HARDINESS Z9–10 H10–9

FLOWERING Early summer

E | *Eucryphia glutinosa* Guindo santo

THIS IS ONE OF THE BEST SHRUBS you can buy. It has toothed, glossy dark green leaves and in mild areas it is semievergreen. Growing to a substantial size, it could almost be called a small tree, and produces a lavish spread of white, sometimes double, 2½in- (6cm-) wide flowers that open in mid- to late summer. The leaves offer a further show of color in the autumn, when they redden as temperatures drop. This is the hardiest of the eucryphias, and does best when the roots are kept in the shade while the top is in the sun. Prune for shape, as necessary, in the spring.

PLANT PROFILE

HEIGHT 30ft (10m)

SPREAD 20ft (6m)

SITE Full sun

SOIL Moist, fertile, free-draining

HARDINESS Z8–11 H12–8

FLOWERING Mid- and late summer

Euonymus europaeus Spindle

MAKING ITS MARK IN THE AUTUMN, when scores of crimson, berrylike capsules split open to reveal tiny orange seeds, this is an excellent deciduous shrub for free-draining soil, especially if it is alkaline. The leaves color up in the autumn, turning purple-red before falling. The very hard wood was used for making spindles for spinning wheels—hence its common name. Plant it in sun to light up the autumn capsules, and prune in late winter. An excellent, treelike alternative is 'Red Cascade', with scarlet autumn foliage.

OTHER VARIETIES *E. alatus* (leaves turn dark red in autumn, reddish purple fruit); *E. japonicus* (white-tinged pink fruit); *E. latifolius* (leaves turn brilliant red in autumn, red fruit); *E. planipes* (red fruit).

PLANT PROFILE	
HEIGHT 10ft (3m)	
SPREAD 10ft (3m)	
SITE Sun or semi-shade	
SOIL Free-draining	
HARDINESS Z4–7	
FLOWERING Late spring	

E

Euonymus fortunei 'Silver Queen' Wintercreeper

EACH LEAF OF THIS HARDY EVERGREEN has a band of white (pale yellow in the spring) around a dark green center. For about 10 days it is covered in tiny greenish white flowers, but a long hot summer is needed if berries are to be produced in any number. When grown against a wall it will turn into a self-clinging climber and shoot up to double its usual height. For good leaf color, full sun is needed, and it will grow in most soils (except very wet). Prune immediately after flowering, when necessary, to control its size and shape.

OTHER VARIETIES *E. fortunei* 'Emerald Gaiety' (compact, white leaf margins turn pink in winter); *E. fortunei* 'Emerald 'n' Gold' (bright yellow leaf margins turn pink in winter).

PLANT PROFILE

HEIGHT 8ft (2.5m)

SPREAD 5ft (1.5m)

SITE Full sun or light shade

SOIL Free-draining

HARDINESS Z5–9 H9–5

FLOWERING Late spring or summer

In midsummer, prune back the flowered stems to a strong shoot or bud low down. Wash your hands after handling this plant, since all parts are toxic.

Euphorbia characias subsp. *wulfenii* Wulfen's spurge

E

DRAMATIC AND SHAPELY, this shrub has long, stiff, erect stems with fingerlike, bluish green leaves, while the flowers are made up of yellow-green, cuplike bracts and purple nectar glands. Grow it as a feature plant or in a large container, but it needs space to be fully appreciated. The soil must be light and free-draining, and it needs a position where it receives protection from icy winds. Cut off the flowered shoots at the base in the summer after blooming and they will be replaced by new, flower-bearing stems the following spring.

OTHER VARIETIES *E. amygdaloides* var. *robbiae* (smaller-growing, reddish green stems); *E. characias* subsp. *wulfenii* 'John Tomlinson' (almost spherical heads of yellow-green flowers).

PLANT PROFILE	
HEIGHT 4ft (1.2m)	
SPREAD 4ft (1.2m)	
SITE Full sun	
SOIL Free-draining	
HARDINESS Z7–11 H12–7	
FLOWERING Spring and early summer	

E

Euryops acraeus Mountain daisy

DWARF AND EYE-CATCHING, this beautiful evergreen shrub produces a profusion of daisylike, deep yellow flowers and makes a compact mound of silver-gray, leathery leaves. An ideal plant for a rock or gravel garden, it is also suitable for a border if given a position right at the front where it can be seen and appreciated. In its native South Africa it grows on mountain slopes where the soil is free-draining and not too fertile. It needs the same conditions in the garden; it will quickly weaken and die if the roots are locked in wet soil over winter. It will also benefit from some shelter against frost.

OTHER VARIETY *E. pectinatus* (taller, bright yellow flowers).

PLANT PROFILE
HEIGHT 12in (30cm)
SPREAD 12in (30cm)
SITE Full sun
SOIL Free-draining
HARDINESS Z9–11 H12–9
FLOWERING Late spring and early summer

Exochorda x *macrantha* 'The Bride' Pearl bush

E

FOR A TERRIFIC DISPLAY OF FLOWERS lasting only about eight days, make sure you are at home at the start of summer. That is when this compact, deciduous shrub puts on an impressive show of pure white blooms held on arching stems. Slow-growing—it puts on just 3ft (1m) of growth in five years—it makes an excellent choice for small gardens. It is also extremely reliable and thrives in most soils except for very wet or shallow, alkaline ground. It is best planted with other shrubs that flower afterward to keep a good show going throughout the summer months.

OTHER VARIETIES *E. giraldii* (taller-growing); *E. giraldii* var. *wilsonii* (white flowers, green-stalked leaves, pinkish green when young).

PLANT PROFILE
HEIGHT 6ft (2m)
SPREAD 10ft (3m)
SITE Full sun or light dappled shade
SOIL Free-draining
HARDINESS Z5–9 H9–5
FLOWERING Late spring and early summer

F

Fabiana imbricata f. *violacea*

THIS BEAUTIFUL, MEDIUM-SIZED, evergreen shrub has upright stems and spreading, horizontal branches. It produces scores of small, white to pale mauve, tubular flowers nestling among the needlelike green leaves, giving a fresh, bright, early summer show. Fabianas need a sunny, sheltered position in order to thrive—for example, at the foot of a wall—with free-draining, neutral to slightly acidic soil. You can also grow it in a rock garden or right at the front of a border, but avoid planting it on thin soil over an alkaline base.

OTHER VARIETIES *F. imbricata* (taller-growing); *F. imbricata* 'Prostrata' (low-growing, white flowers).

PLANT PROFILE	
HEIGHT 3ft (1m)	
SPREAD 6ft (2m)	
SITE Full sun	
SOIL Fertile, free-draining	
HARDINESS Z9–11 H12–10	
FLOWERING Early summer	

Fallopia baldschuanica Russian vine

F

THIS IS A NO-NONSENSE, rampant, fast-spreading deciduous climber with clusters of white flowers in the second half of summer. It is perfectly happy in moderately fertile or even poor soil, as long as it has good drainage, and requires pruning after flowering only if you need to restrain it and prevent it from getting out of hand. You can either train this climber up a sturdy old tree or allow it to form a huge mound over a tree stump. Impressive, but not the neatest of plants, it is best grown in a wild or informal garden, far away from anything that might be overwhelmed.

PLANT PROFILE
HEIGHT 40ft (12m)
SITE Full sun or partial shade
SOIL Average, free-draining
HARDINESS Z5–9 H9–5
FLOWERING Late summer and autumn

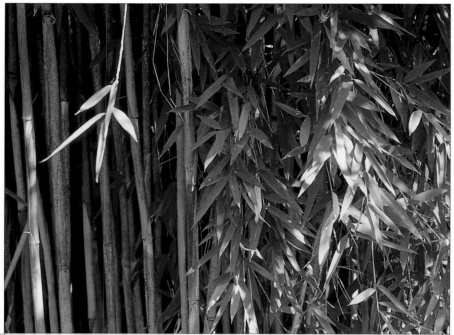

Fargesia nitida Bamboo

EXTREMELY TOUGH AND GRACEFUL, this bamboo is slow-growing, clump-forming and noninvasive. It forms a tall, dense thicket and is therefore best grown as a perimeter hedge in a wild or woodland garden, or as a feature within a very large lawn. The evergreen leaves are dark green, but they do not appear until the second year, leaving the beautiful purple-green canes exposed, creating a stunning effect. There are several good forms of *Fargesia nitida*, including the small-leaved 'Eisenach' and elegant 'Nymphenburg'.

OTHER VARIETIES *F. murielae* (powdery white canes turn yellow-green, then all green); *F. murielae* 'Jumbo' (smaller-growing, larger leaves); *F. murielae* 'Simba' (compact, good for small gardens).

PLANT PROFILE
HEIGHT To 15ft (5m)
SPREAD 5ft (1.5m) or more
SITE Partial or light shade
SOIL Moist, fertile
HARDINESS Z5–9 H9–5

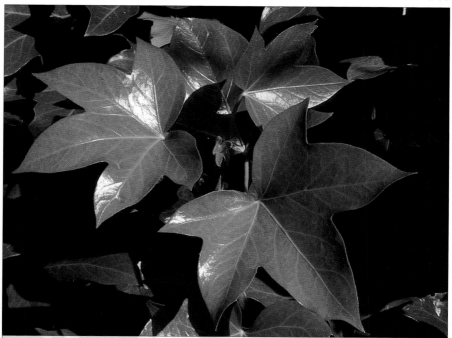

x *Fatshedera lizei* Tree-ivy

F

SPLENDID, JUNGLY, AND SPRAWLING, this cross between an ivy and a fatsia makes a climbing evergreen shrub with shiny leaves up to 10in (25cm) long. The greenish white flowers appear late in the season and are quite insignificant. Good for livening up an unused, slightly shady corner, it is quite unfussy and thrives in a wide range of conditions, although shelter is a must to keep the leaves from being ruined by cold winds. Pruning is unnecessary except when growth creates an unbalanced shape. 'Variegata' is even more striking.

OTHER VARIETY x *F. lizei* 'Variegata' (leaves with narrow, creamy-white margins).

PLANT PROFILE

HEIGHT 4–6ft (1.2–2m) or more

SPREAD 10ft (3m)

SITE Full sun or partial shade

SOIL Fertile, moist but free-draining

HARDINESS Z8–11 H12–8

FLOWERING Autumn

F

Fatsia japonica Japanese aralia

DRAMATIC AND ARCHITECTURAL, this evergreen adds a sculptural element to any garden. Also known as the fig-leafed palm and the false castor bean, it will even add shape to a shady corner with its mass of junglelike, deeply cut, shiny leaves, each about 12in (30cm) wide. It has a spreading habit, which means it can be easily underplanted with shade-loving plants, including ferns, hostas, and snowdrops. If the aralia becomes too tall and multibranched (when, incidentally, the leaves become smaller and less dramatic), ruthlessly cut back the main stem and new stems will soon regrow. In other circumstances, pruning is unnecessary.

PLANT PROFILE

HEIGHT 5–12ft (1.5–4m)

SPREAD 5–12ft (1.5–4m)

SITE Full sun or light dappled shade

SOIL Moist, fertile, free-draining

HARDINESS Z8–11 H12–8

FLOWERING Autumn

Forsythia x *intermedia* 'Lynwood'

PROVIDING A COLORFUL NOTE in spring, when the bare, upright
stems of forsythias are smothered in rich yellow flowers, 'Lynwood'
makes a fine hedge when used alone or with evergreens. You can
also snip off the top of the flowering stems for cut-flower displays,
or strip the leaves from longer stems in summer and use them to
support floppy perennials. It grows in any soil (ideally well-drained),
and the more sun it gets, the better the flowering. Prune after it has
flowered, and cut down old stems of mature plants to the ground.

OTHER VARIETIES *F.* 'Beatrix Farrand' (taller-growing, pale yellow
flowers); *F.* 'Golden Nugget' (golden-yellow flowers); *F. suspensa* (clusters
of yellow flowers, mid- to dark green leaves).

PLANT PROFILE
HEIGHT 10ft (3m)
SPREAD 10ft (3m)
SITE Full sun
SOIL Free-draining
HARDINESS Z6–9 H9–6
FLOWERING Early and midspring

F

Fothergilla major

MASSES OF SWEETLY SCENTED white or pink-tinged flowers at the start of the growing season, and fabulous autumn color, when the shiny dark green leaves turn red, orange and yellow, are the chief assets of this slow-growing, deciduous North American shrub. The flowers, interestingly, do not have any petals, only bristling stamens. Make sure that the shrub is planted in full sun if you want the best autumn color and abundant flowers. The soil needs to be acidic, with plenty of well-rotted compost added to the planting hole.

OTHER VARIETIES   *F. gardenii* (smaller-growing, white flowers, bright red, orange, and yellow autumn leaf color); *F. gardenii* 'Blue Mist' (blue-green leaves).

PLANT PROFILE

HEIGHT 8ft (2.5m)

SPREAD 6ft (2m)

SITE Full sun or partial shade

SOIL Acidic, moist but free-draining

HARDINESS Z4–8 H9–2

FLOWERING Late spring and early summer

Fremontodendron 'California Glory' Flannel bush

F

OBTAINING A BIG, SHOWY DISPLAY of bright yellow flowers—each about 2in (5cm) wide—from this evergreen North American shrub depends on two factors. First, it needs a warm, sunny, protective wall in all but the mildest gardens, and second, you must provide it with relatively poor to moderately fertile soil with good drainage. Once it is established and growing, it needs to be trained along horizontal wires. It grows at a rate of about 12in (30cm) a year until it reaches its ultimate height, when it makes an impressive sight.

OTHER VARIETIES *F. californicum* (saucer-shaped, yellow flowers, dark green leaves); *F.* 'Pacific Sunset' (bright yellow flowers in summer with long, slender-pointed lobes).

PLANT PROFILE
HEIGHT 20ft (6m)
SPREAD 12ft (4m)
SITE Full sun
SOIL Average, free-draining
HARDINESS Z8–11 H12–8
FLOWERING Late spring to midautumn

F

Fuchsia 'Genii'

THIS VERSATILE SHRUB can be grown as part of a flowering hedge, as a border plant, in an ornamental container (to be brought indoors in winter), or as a standard. 'Genii' is erect, deciduous, and bushy, and is in flower nearly all summer. It needs shelter and protection in colder regions, plus a thick winter mulch of compost, and plants should be cut back in the spring to encourage new, bushy growth. Grow it in free-draining, rich soil, and water young plants well in their first year as they are getting established.

OTHER VARIETIES *F.* 'Brookwood Belle' (cerise and white double flowers); *F.* 'Display' (carmine and pink single flowers); *F.* 'Riccartonii' (small scarlet and purple flowers).

PLANT PROFILE
HEIGHT 3ft (1m)
SPREAD 3ft (1m)
SITE Full sun
SOIL Fertile, free-draining
HARDINESS Z9–11 H12–9
FLOWERING Summer

Garrya elliptica Silk-tassel bush

G

TOUGH AND INDESTRUCTIBLE, this evergreen shrub looks best from midwinter to early spring, when it is covered by long, dangling, gray-green catkins. The shrub also makes an excellent, dense, bushy hedge, and can be easily kept in shape with a trim once the display of catkins is over. Given free-draining soil, *Garrya elliptica* also grows well in coastal gardens, but do not use it as a windbreak because it likes a sheltered position. Double-check that you are buying male plants because these provide showier catkins than females.

OTHER VARIETIES *G. elliptica* 'James Roof' (male, longer catkins); *G.* x *issaquahensis* 'Pat Ballard' (smaller-growing, purple-tinged catkins).

PLANT PROFILE

HEIGHT 12ft (4m)

SPREAD 12ft (4m)

SITE Full sun or partial shade

SOIL Free-draining

HARDINESS Z8–11 H12–8

FLOWERING Midwinter to early spring

G

Gaultheria mucronata 'Mulberry Wine' Prickly heath

THIS COMPACT, VIGOROUS EVERGREEN (formerly known as *Pernettya mucronata*) is popular for its reddish young stems and glossy foliage. The white, late-spring flowers might be minuscule, but they appear in numbers large enough to give a good display. These are followed by its chief asset (if you have an adjacent male and female)—masses of magenta fruit, ripening to dark purple. It grows best in partial shade, and needs moist soil that is peaty and acidic.

OTHER VARIETIES *G. cuneata* (smaller-growing, white flowers followed by white fruit); *G. mucronata* 'Cherry Ripe' (bright cerise fruit); *G. mucronata* 'Snow White' (white fruit slightly spotted with pink); *G. shallon* (pink-tinged white flowers, purple fruit).

PLANT PROFILE	
HEIGHT	4ft (1.2m)
SPREAD	4ft (1.2m)
SITE	Partial shade
SOIL	Acidic, moist
HARDINESS	Z8–9 H9–8
FLOWERING	Late spring

Gaultheria procumbens Checkerberry

G

WITH ITS LOW, SPREADING GROWTH, the checkerberry makes ideal ground cover. It is vigorous, however, and shouldn't be grown too close to neighboring plants. The glossy, dark green leaves release a sweet, gentle scent when torn, and the summer flowers are up to 1in (2.5cm) long. The white or pale pink blooms are then followed by attractive scarlet berries that hang on through the winter. It thrives in peaty, moist, acidic soil and a shady site. Don't be tempted to plant it in the sun unless the soil is damp and never dries out.

OTHER VARIETY *G. mucronata* (taller-growing, white flowers, purple-red to white fruit).

PLANT PROFILE
HEIGHT 6in (15cm)
SPREAD To 3ft (1m) or more
SITE Shade
SOIL Acidic, moist
HARDINESS Z3–8 H8–1
FLOWERING Summer

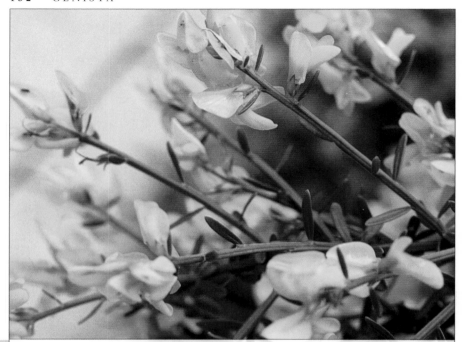

Genista lydia Broom

WHILE MOST BROOMS ARE LARGE, upright shrubs, this low-growing, domed form is a real beauty for rock gardens or raised beds, and is also perfect for the top of a wall, where its gray-green arching stems will tumble over the edge. In early summer it becomes smothered in tiny, pealike, yellow flowers and is so floriferous that you can barely see the blue-green deciduous leaves. Light, free-draining soil is essential; average fertility is fine. No pruning is necessary—if the plant becomes too straggly, simply replace it with a new, young one.

OTHER VARIETIES *G. aetnensis* (treelike, golden yellow flowers); *G. pilosa* 'Vancouver Gold' (mound-forming, yellow flowers); *G. tinctoria* 'Royal Gold' (more upright, yellow flowers in long panicles).

PLANT PROFILE
HEIGHT 24in (60cm)
SPREAD 3ft (1m)
SITE Full sun
SOIL Light to average, free-draining
HARDINESS Z6–9 H9–3
FLOWERING Early summer

Grevillea 'Canberra Gem' Spider flower

THIS QUICK-GROWING EVERGREEN makes a dense, bushy shrub with curiously curly, waxy pink-red flowers. The first buds start to open in late winter and offer a welcome splash of color at such a dull time of year. Flowering then continues well into summer. This Australian native needs a sunny, sheltered site—for example, at the foot of a sunny wall—or grow it in a large tub and bring it under cover over winter. Keep the soil quite dry in winter. Prune for shape after flowering, but avoid contact with your skin because the sap can cause an allergic reaction.

OTHER VARIETY *G. rosmarinifolia* (pink or cream flowers).

PLANT PROFILE
HEIGHT 6–12ft (2–4m)
SPREAD 6–15ft (2–5m)
SITE Full sun
SOIL Acidic to neutral, free-draining
HARDINESS Z9–11 H12–9
FLOWERING Late winter to late summer, often at other times

G | *Grindelia chiloensis* Gumweed

THE ONLY POSSIBLE PROBLEM WITH *Grindelia chiloensis* is that in a cold snap, this sprawling, evergreen shrub will behave more like a perennial, with the topgrowth dying back. If this happens, don't worry; new shoots will appear the following spring. It produces grayish green, 5in– (12cm–) long leaves, and bears attractive, sunny yellow, daisylike blooms on long stalks all through the summer period. This colorful show often extends well into autumn. For the best results, grow it in the sunniest spot in the garden—a hot, dry bank would be perfect—and plant in free-draining, average soil.

PLANT PROFILE
HEIGHT 3ft (1m)
SPREAD 3ft (1m)
SITE Full sun
SOIL Poor to average, free-draining
HARDINESS Z11–15 H12–9
FLOWERING Summer

Griselinia littoralis 'Variegata' Broadleaf

AN EXCELLENT CHOICE for seaside gardens, this plant not only withstands salty winds but benefits from the mild coastal conditions. With its dense, evergreen, apple green leaves with creamy white margins, it is also suitable for gardens that require year-round architectural interest or areas of attractive hedging. The striking foliage makes a contrasting backdrop for the vivid primary colors of a wide range of perennials. The greenish spring flowers are, by contrast, rather inconspicuous. Plant it in fertile, free-draining soil, and prune for shape after flowering.

OTHER VARIETY *G. littoralis* (taller, sometimes treelike in mild areas, apple green leaves).

PLANT PROFILE
HEIGHT 10ft (3m)
SPREAD 6ft (2m)
SITE Full sun
SOIL Light, fertile, free-draining
HARDINESS Z8–9 H9–8
FLOWERING Late spring

H | x *Halimiocistus sahucii* Rock rose

BRIEF ENCOUNTERS OFTEN MAKE a great impression. The charming white flowers of this sun-loving plant from southern France open in the morning only to fade by sunset, but this is certainly not a problem. From early summer there is always a plentiful supply of buds waiting to open on the low, wiry stems, ensuring a good show. To thrive, this low, spreading Mediterranean evergreen needs shelter from winter winds and poor to average, sharply drained soil. Raised beds, gravel and rock gardens, or gaps between the paving on a sunny terrace are all perfect sites.

OTHER VARIETY x *H. wintonensis* 'Merrist Wood Cream' (pale yellow flowers with a red inner band).

PLANT PROFILE
HEIGHT 18in (45cm)
SPREAD 3ft (1m)
SITE Full sun
SOIL Poor to average, sandy, free-draining
HARDINESS Z7–9 H9–7
FLOWERING Summer

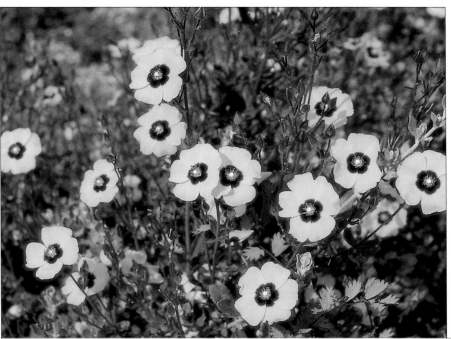

Halimium 'Susan' Rock rose

H

THE RICHLY COLORED, bright yellow flowers of this low-growing, spreading shrub have a red-purple ring right in the middle. Like all halimiums, it needs all the summer sun it can get, plus average, free-draining, dryish soil with some shelter. Take care when siting this plant because it hates being disturbed once it is established. A good choice for the front of a border or a large rock garden, it also makes an excellent container plant. If plants start to look straggly, give them a light trim for shape in spring.

OTHER VARIETIES *H. lasianthum* (slightly larger, golden-yellow flowers with brown centers); *H. ocymoides* (taller-growing, golden yellow flowers with black-purple centers, downy gray-green leaves).

PLANT PROFILE
HEIGHT 18in (45cm)
SPREAD 24in (60cm)
SITE Full sun
SOIL Moderately fertile, sandy, free-draining
HARDINESS Z9–11 H12–9
FLOWERING Summer

H | *Hamamelis* x *intermedia* 'Pallida' Witch hazel

HIGHLY RATED, this spreading, deciduous winter shrub is barnacled with large, sulfur yellow flowers. Looking more like short tufts of yellow string than a traditional flower, they carry a delightfully sweet fragrance. 'Pallida' is fairly large—really more of a rounded tree than a shrub—and needs a woodland garden or a site on the boundary of a medium-sized garden. A fairly sheltered spot in slightly acidic to neutral, moist but free-draining soil suits it best. Prune for shape only in spring.

OTHER VARIETIES *H.* x *intermedia* 'Arnold Promise' (large yellow flowers); *H.* x *intermedia* 'Diane' (dark red flowers, yellow and red autumn foliage); *H.* x *intermedia* 'Jelena' (coppery orange flowers).

PLANT PROFILE
HEIGHT 12ft (4m)
SPREAD 12ft (4m)
SITE Full sun or partial shade
SOIL Acidic to neutral, fertile, moist but free-draining
HARDINESS Z5–9 H9–1
FLOWERING Early and midwinter

Hebe 'Great Orme'

H

LOOKING EQUALLY GOOD in a border or a large container, this hebe makes a rounded evergreen with shiny leaves. The flowers appear in the second half of summer and continue into autumn; when they first open, the flowers are pink, but they age to white. Like most hebes, 'Great Orme' needs a sheltered spot with protection from cold winds, and average, well-drained soil. Bring potgrown plants into a frost-free greenhouse over winter. Prune to shape in spring.

OTHER VARIETIES *H. albicans* (smaller-growing, white flowers); *H. cupressoides* 'Boughton Dome' (dwarf, pale green, scalelike leaves); *H.* 'Midsummer Beauty' (taller-growing, lilac-purple flowers).

PLANT PROFILE
HEIGHT 4ft (1.2m)
SPREAD 4ft (1.2m)
SITE Sun or partial shade
SOIL Average, moist but free-draining
HARDINESS Z9–11 H12–9
FLOWERING Midsummer to midautumn

LIGHT PRUNING

First, completely cut out any frost-damaged stems. Then lightly trim the whole plant with shears to stimulate new growth.

H *Hebe pinguifolia* 'Pagei'

MOST PEOPLE THINK OF HEBES AS ROUNDED, but 'Pagei' is a prostrate shrub that makes excellent ground cover. Grow it in borders, as an edging for paths, and in rock gardens. The bright white flowers are offset by small, round, blue-green leaves. Free-draining soil and shelter from cold winds are essential, and if you wish to prune your hebe to make it more shapely, do so in early spring. As well as crisp white, hebes come in a vast range of colors, including blues, pinks, purples, and reds.

OTHER VARIETIES *H. albicans* (compact mound, white flowers); *H. hulkeana* (taller-growing, lavender-blue, lilac, or white flowers).

PLANT PROFILE	
HEIGHT 12in (30cm)	
SPREAD 3ft (1m)	
SITE Sun or partial shade	
SOIL Average, free-draining	
HARDINESS Z8–10 H10–8	
FLOWERING Late spring and early summer	

Hedera colchica 'Sulphur Heart' Ivy

ONE OF THE BEST VARIEGATED IVIES, 'Sulphur Heart' is a bold, dramatic evergreen climber. The light green leaves, up to 6in (15cm) long, make a colorful splash with their creamy yellow markings. A rampant spreader, it will quickly cover ugly sheds, walls, and fences, but if you are thinking of training it on a house wall, make sure that the surface is in very good condition, since the self-clinging suckers could cause damage. Cut it back in spring if it spreads beyond its allotted space and into gutters, window frames, or under roof shingles. Avoid planting in heavy, wet soil.

OTHER VARIETIES *H. colchica* 'Dentata' (purple-flushed stems); *H. colchica* 'Dentata Variegata' (white-margined, mottled gray-green leaves).

PLANT PROFILE

HEIGHT 15ft (5m)

SITE Sun

SOIL Fertile, free-draining

HARDINESS Z6–11 H12–1

FLOWERING Autumn

H | *Hedera helix* 'Glacier' Common ivy

A VIGOROUS IVY, SUCH AS 'GLACIER', will quickly cloak a small shed or ugly wall with its attractive variegated leaves. Without training, the plant naturally forms a ground-hugging mound, so you need to entice the self-clinging stems to grow upward for the first few years. You can also train it as a standard by growing it up a sturdy post topped with a ball-shaped wire frame. Note that variegated ivies must be grown in full sun or they will lose their markings. Plant in average soil.

OTHER VARIETIES *H. helix* 'Buttercup' (yellow leaves in full sun, pale green leaves in shade); *H. helix* 'Cavendishii' (creamy yellow leaf margins); *H. helix* 'Pedata' (leaves are shaped like a bird's foot).

PLANT PROFILE
HEIGHT 6ft (2m) or more
SITE Sun
SOIL Average
HARDINESS Z5–11 H12–6
FLOWERING Autumn

Helianthemum 'Raspberry Ripple' Rock rose

H

IDEAL AS GROUNDCOVER for rock or gravel gardens, this small evergreen stands out with its white flowers, each with a yellow eye and purple-pink markings radiating from the center. Like other rock roses, it's not too fussy and grows in average, free-draining soil, although a sunny situation is essential for it to thrive. After flowering, cut back flowered shoots to within 1in (2.5cm) of the previous year's growth. Rock roses are available in a wide range of colors.

OTHER VARIETIES *H.* 'Chocolate Blotch' (buff-colored flowers with chocolate brown markings); *H.* 'Fire Dragon' (vivid orange-red flowers); *H.* 'The Bride' (white flowers); *H.* 'Wisley Primrose' (pale primrose yellow flowers).

PLANT PROFILE
HEIGHT 8in (20cm)
SPREAD 12in (30cm)
SITE Full sun
SOIL Average, free-draining
HARDINESS Z6–8 H8–6
FLOWERING Late spring to midsummer

H | *Helichrysum italicum* subsp. *serotinum* Curry plant

CRUSH THE AROMATIC LEAVES of the curry plant and you'll discover why it is so named. It is often planted as a mini-hedge in the border or herb garden, where its silver-gray, evergreen foliage is a restful color break between other plants. It makes a wonderfully bushy shrub and is studded with dark yellow flowers throughout summer. For the curry plant to thrive, you must plant it in quick-draining soil in a sheltered spot—cold, drying winds and excessive winter moisture will be fatal. To maintain shape, in spring cut back flowered shoots to within 1in (2.5cm) of the previous year's growth.

OTHER VARIETIES *H. italicum* (larger, dark yellow flowers); *H. petiolare* (woolly gray leaves); *H. splendidum* (larger, white stems, yellow flowers).

PLANT PROFILE
HEIGHT 16in (40cm)
SPREAD 30in (75cm)
SITE Full sun
SOIL Average, free-draining
HARDINESS Z7–10 H10–7
FLOWERING Summer to autumn

Hibiscus syriacus 'Oiseau Bleu' Blue Bird rose of Sharon

H

HIBISCUS ARE COLORFUL PLANTS with flowers in shades of white through to deep purple, but the bright blue of 'Oiseau Bleu' takes some beating. Try growing two contrasting-colored plants together, allowing their flowers to intermingle. *Hibiscus syriacus* is a hardy, deciduous shrub that performs best in rich, moist but well-drained soil. Full sun isn't an option, it's a necessity, and the hotter the summer, the better flowering will be. Prune when young to encourage bushiness, but thereafter, pruning is not needed.

OTHER VARIETIES *H. syriacus* 'Diana' (very large white flowers); *H. syriacus* 'Pink Giant' (large red-centered pink flowers); *H. syriacus* 'Red Heart' (red-centered white flowers).

PLANT PROFILE		
HEIGHT 10ft (3m)		
SPREAD 6ft (2m)		
SITE Full sun		
SOIL Fertile, moist but free-draining		
HARDINESS Z5–9 H9–5		
FLOWERING Late summer to midautumn		

H

Hippophae rhamnoides Sea buckthorn

ESSENTIAL IN ANY EXPOSED COASTAL GARDEN, the sea buckthorn happily tolerates gales and thin, sandy soil, creating a highly effective summer windbreak. In winter, however, because it is deciduous it will lose its protecting thicket of gray-green leaves. The advantage of growing a few plants together is that you can mix males among the female plants so that they will produce their bright orange berries. Because birds dislike the bitter taste of the fruit, they are left untouched over winter to give the hedge a bit of color. Pruning is usually unnecessary, but to improve overall shapeliness, you can cut out badly congested or wayward stems in late summer.

OTHER VARIETY *H. rhamnoides* 'Leikora' (very profuse berries).

PLANT PROFILE
HEIGHT 20ft (6m)
SPREAD 20ft (6m)
SITE Full sun
SOIL Moist but free-draining, preferably sandy
HARDINESS Z3–8 H8–1
FLOWERING Spring

Hoheria glabrata Mountain ribbonwood

AN ATTRACTIVE FOCAL POINT in a woodland garden or the center of a spacious lawn, it's hardly surprising that this impressive, vigorous deciduous shrub is often listed as a tree. In the first half of summer the arching stems are tightly packed with scented, white flowers (*see inset*) that are attractive to butterflies. It is not usually planted away from coastal sites, which is a shame because it thrives in sheltered, sunny gardens in any mild region where the soil is free-draining. If the topgrowth dies back in winter, new shoots should appear from the base the following spring.

OTHER VARIETY *H. sexstylosa* (evergreen, white flowers).

PLANT PROFILE	
HEIGHT 22ft (7m)	
SPREAD 22ft (7m)	
SITE Sun or partial shade	
SOIL Average, free-draining	
HARDINESS Z9–10 H10–9	
FLOWERING Midsummer	

H

Holboellia coriacea Sausage vine

ONE OF THE BEST and also one of the most underrated climbers, *Holboellia coriacea* is an evergreen vine with heavenly, fragrant flowers. To help its woody stems climb, it needs a strong frame, such as a wall strung with horizontal wires, or a sturdy tree trunk. The male flowers, which appear on the previous year's growth, are mauve, while the greenish white females are produced on current growth. After a hot summer, purple fruit may be produced. Provide free-draining, rich soil and a sunny, sheltered site. Pruning is not essential.

OTHER VARIETY *H. latifolia* (shorter-growing, white male and purple female flowers).

PLANT PROFILE
HEIGHT 22ft (7m)
SITE Full sun or partial shade
SOIL Fertile, free-draining
HARDINESS Z10–11 H12–10
FLOWERING Spring

Holodiscus discolor Ocean spray

H

THIS GIANT, UPRIGHT, ARCHING SHRUB is usually planted on the perimeter of a garden. In midsummer, its long gray-green leaves are almost hidden by an eruption of creamy white, cup-shaped flowers that hang in airy, plumelike sprays up to 12in (30cm) long. Pruning is usually unnecessary, but after flowering, you can help to reinvigorate mature plants and encourage them to produce new shoots by cutting out one in four of the old stems to a healthy bud on lower growth. For ocean spray to reach its full potential, it must have a rich, moist but free-draining soil in sun or light shade.

PLANT PROFILE
HEIGHT 12ft (4m)
SPREAD 12ft (4m)
SITE Sun or partial shade
SOIL Fertile, moist but free-draining
HARDINESS Z6–9 H9–6
FLOWERING Midsummer

H

Humulus lupulus 'Aureus' Hop

HOPS ARE FAST-CLIMBING PERENNIALS that shoot up in spring. 'Aureus' produces a bright summery mass of large, yellow-green leaves and looks wonderful grown over a pergola, against a wall or fence, between other climbers, or up a tall tree. A good support is essential to stop topgrowth from being damaged in blustery winds. The flowers on female plants mature into 2in- (5cm-) long hops. Fertile, moist but free-draining soil is best, and for the brightest leaf color, grow it in full sun. As a screen it will only be effective in summer because the plant dies down during the winter.

OTHER VARIETY *H. lupulus* (light green leaves, fragrant, green female flowers become straw-colored).

PLANT PROFILE
HEIGHT 20ft (6m)
SITE Sun or partial shade
SOIL Fertile, moist but free-draining
HARDINESS Z4–8 H8–1
FLOWERING Summer

Hydrangea anomala subsp. *petiolaris* Climbing hydrangea

H

LOOKING NOTHING LIKE the ornamental hydrangeas typically found in borders, this woody-stemmed deciduous climber will quickly cover a huge stretch of wall or climb up into a solid, mature tree, clinging with its strong aerial roots. If you prefer, it is also sturdy enough to be grown as a freestanding shrub or bush. It makes a superb mass of dark green leaves, up to 4½in (11cm) long, which turn yellow in autumn before falling. The creamy white flowers last only two to three weeks in summer. It performs best in sun but will cope well with cool shade. Prune after flowering if the plant is in danger of outgrowing the available space.

PLANT PROFILE

HEIGHT 50ft (15m)

SITE Sun or partial shade

SOIL Fertile, moist but free-draining

HARDINESS Z4–9 H9–1

FLOWERING Summer

H *Hydrangea macrophylla* 'Ayesha'

A CURIOUSLY BEAUTIFUL HYDRANGEA, 'Ayesha' has flowers like those of a lilac (*Syringa*) and glossy leaves. Soil chemistry affects all the macrophylla types: on acidic soil their flowers are lilac, while on other soils they come up pink—only the whites stay the same color. Shelter from cold, drying winds is important, as is moist but free-draining soil. Annual pruning will improve the show of flowers: cut mature plants back hard in spring to a couple of vigorous buds, removing one-third of each stem. Skin contact can trigger allergies.

OTHER VARIETIES *H. macrophylla* 'Blue Bonnet' (rich blue to pink flowers); *H. macrophylla* 'Europa' (dark pink to purple-blue flowers); *H. macrophylla* 'White Wave' (white sterile and pink to blue fertile flowers).

PLANT PROFILE	
HEIGHT 5ft (1.5m)	
SPREAD 6ft (2m)	
SITE Sun or partial shade	
SOIL Fertile, moist but free-draining	
HARDINESS Z6–9 H9–6	
FLOWERING Mid- and late summer	

Hydrangea paniculata 'Grandiflora'

THIS ORNAMENTAL DECIDUOUS HYDRANGEA is one of the best, with large flowerheads up to 12in (30cm) tall. They open pure white but soon acquire a pink tinge. Prune in the spring to within a few buds of the woody framework to encourage even larger flowerheads. 'Grandiflora' needs to be grown toward the back of a spacious border, where the heavy blooms can droop forward unhampered, particularly after rain. Grow in rich, moist but well-drained soil, and protect from cold, drying winds.

OTHER VARIETIES   *H. paniculata* 'Floribunda' (pink-tinged white sterile flowers); *H. paniculata* 'Kyushu' (glossy leaves); *H. paniculata* 'Praecox' (flowers earlier, from midsummer).

PLANT PROFILE
HEIGHT 10–22ft (3–7m)
SPREAD 8ft (2.5m)
SITE Sun or partial shade
SOIL Fertile, moist but free-draining
HARDINESS Z3–8 H8–1
FLOWERING Late summer and early autumn

H | *Hydrangea serrata* 'Bluebird'

IF YOU WANT A DECIDUOUS HYDRANGEA that is compact, erect, and never gets too large, choose 'Bluebird'. It is reliably hardy and will withstand severe spring frosts. The prolific displays of flattish flowerheads will be rich blue on acidic soil and reddish purple on alkaline ground. The flowers dry particularly well for indoor arrangements. The shrub has a final fling in autumn, when its foliage reddens up before falling. For best results grow it in rich, moist but well-drained soil in a spot that's sheltered from cold, drying winds.

OTHER VARIETIES *H. macrophylla* (taller-growing); *H.* 'Preziosa' (small heads of white flowers); *H. quercifolia* (taller-growing, mound-forming, pink-tinged white flowers, green leaves turn bronze-purple).

PLANT PROFILE

HEIGHT 4ft (1.2m)

SPREAD 4ft (1.2m)

SITE Sun or partial shade

SOIL Fertile, moist but free-draining

HARDINESS Z6–9 H9–6

FLOWERING Summer to autumn

Hypericum 'Hidcote' St. John's wort

HIGHLY EFFECTIVE AND PERFECTLY RELIABLE, this shrub can be grown in a wide range of gardens given average to fertile, free-draining soil. It is just the right size for most borders and, as well as a prolific show of flowers, provides a dense covering of glossy, evergreen leaves. The butter yellow, five-petaled blooms appear in the second half of summer. Prune lightly to shape after flowering.

OTHER VARIETIES *H. calycinum* (shorter, wide-spreading); *H. forrestii* (mid-green leaves turning red in late autumn); *H. kouytchense* (flowers followed by red fruit, bluish green leaves); *H.* 'Rowallane' (taller, golden yellow flowers late summer to autumn, semievergreen).

PLANT PROFILE	
HEIGHT 4ft (1.2m)	
SPREAD 5ft (1.5m)	
SITE Sun or partial shade	
SOIL Average, moist but free-draining	
HARDINESS Z6–9 H9–6	
FLOWERING Midsummer to early autumn	

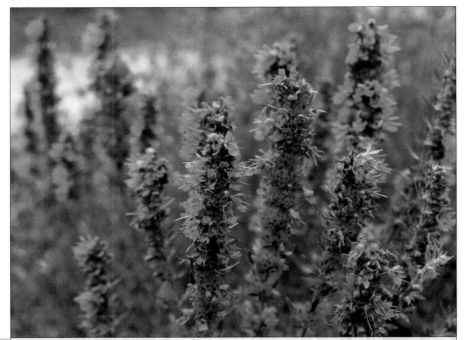

H

Hyssopus officinalis Hyssop

THE CHIEF VIRTUE of this aromatic, semievergreen shrub is its dark blue, mid– to late-season flowers, which are a magnet for bees and butterflies. A versatile herb from southern Europe, it offers flowers for salads, and leaves for cooking, potpourri, and infusions (although pregnant women should avoid it in any form). It also makes a beautiful border plant when grown as a miniature hedge to divide up a large bed. A sun lover, it must also have light, free-draining soil. In spring, clip it lightly for shape with shears, or cut back hard to renovate.

OTHER VARIETIES *H. officinalis* f. *albus* (white flowers); *H. officinalis* subsp. *aristatus* (dense, upright, bright green leaves); *H. officinalis* 'Roseus' (pink flowers).

PLANT PROFILE
HEIGHT 24in (60cm)
SPREAD 3ft (1m)
SITE Full sun
SOIL Light, free-draining
HARDINESS Z6–9 H9–6
FLOWERING Midsummer to early autumn

Ilex aquifolium 'Handsworth New Silver' Common holly

I

THE SPINY, DARK GREEN LEAVES of this evergreen shrub or tree have attractive creamy margins. Note that 'Handsworth New Silver' is a female holly and will bear cheery bright red berries, following cross-pollination from a nearby male. Likely males include the rather confusingly named 'Golden Queen' and 'Silver Queen'. Hollies can be grown as individual specimens or hedges, or be topiarized—pruning for shape should be done in early spring. Plant in full sun or light shade for the strongest variegation.

OTHER VARIETIES *I. aquifolium* 'Argentea Marginata' (female, cream-streaked leaves with white margins, red berries); *I. aquifolium* 'Madame Briot' (female, purple stems, gold-margined leaves, red fruit).

PLANT PROFILE
HEIGHT 25ft (8m)
SPREAD 15ft (5m)
SITE Full sun
SOIL Moist but free-draining
HARDINESS Z7–9 H9–7
FLOWERING Spring to early summer

HARD PRUNING

In warm areas, very little pruning is required, but in cold gardens the stems can be damaged by frost and are best cut to near ground level in spring.

I *Indigofera heterantha* Himalayan indigo

THIS VERSATILE DECIDUOUS SHRUB shrub manages to pull something out of the hat to sustain interest nearly year-round. It's a winning mix of arching branches with fernlike leaves and pretty, pealike, purple-pink flowers that appear over a long season. It prefers a sunny, sheltered site, but at the end of winter, don't be alarmed to see it cut down by the freezing temperatures, because it will reshoot. If you want to restrict its size, cut stems back down to the ground each spring to force up new flowering shoots. In a romantic or cottage garden setting, *Indigofera heterantha* will be a star.

OTHER VARIETIES *I. amblyantha* (pink flowers); *I. kirilowii* (smaller-growing, rose pink flowers).

PLANT PROFILE

HEIGHT 6–10ft (2–3m)

SPREAD 6–10ft (2–3m)

SITE Full sun

SOIL Moist but free-draining

HARDINESS Z6–9 H9–6

FLOWERING Early summer to early autumn

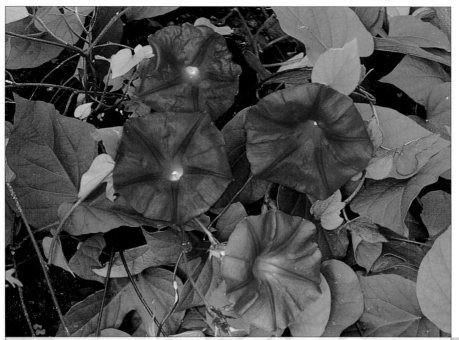

Ipomoea indica Blue dawn flower

I

WINTER WARMTH IS NEEDED to keep this climber growing all year; if you're going to plant it outdoors in cooler regions, treat it as an annual and discard it at the end of summer. A vigorous twiner, it will grow up horizontal wires against a conservatory wall, or over a wigwam of canes or a pergola in the garden. The flowers are a sumptuous rich blue with a hint of regal purple, but individual blooms don't last long, opening in the morning and dying by the end of the day. In season, however, new buds are always waiting to open in rapid succession.

OTHER VARIETIES *I. nil* 'Scarlett O'Hara' (bright red flowers); *I. tricolor* 'Crimson Rambler' (smaller-growing, red flowers with white throats); *I. tricolor* 'Heavenly Blue' (azure flowers with white throats).

PLANT PROFILE

HEIGHT 20ft (6m) or more

SITE Full sun

SOIL Fertile, free-draining

HARDINESS Z12–15 H12–9

FLOWERING Late spring to autumn

I

Itea ilicifolia Sweetspire

THERE'S SOMETHING IRRESISTIBLE about honey-scented flowers, and the thin, dangling catkins of *Itea ilicifolia*, which can grow to 12in (30cm) long, are particularly sweet. Grow this evergreen shrub as a feature plant or hedge, or train it against a wall as a living climbing frame for clematis. Plant it somewhere sheltered because cold winter winds will damage the hollylike foliage. Grow in reasonably fertile, moist soil—young plants will need watering during dry spells, since their roots take a while to become established. In spring, a thick mulch of compost after watering or heavy rain will seal in moisture.

OTHER VARIETY *I. virginica* (shorter-growing, fragrant, white flowers, prefers slightly acidic soil in partial shade).

PLANT PROFILE	
HEIGHT 10–15ft (3–5m)	
SPREAD 10ft (3m)	
SITE Full sun	
SOIL Fertile, moist but free-draining	
HARDINESS Z7–9 H9–6	
FLOWERING Midsummer to early autumn	

Jasminum nudiflorum Winter jasmine

J

THE UNDISPUTED STAR OF THE WINTER GARDEN, *Jasminum nudiflorum*
produces a flash of bright yellow on bare stems long before there
is any hint of spring in the air. The deciduous leaves won't appear
until the flowers fade. The thin, arching stems are easily trained
against a wall or fence to create a fan of flowers, and you can jazz
up the effect by planting it beside a red-berrying cotoneaster.
Winter jasmine is a remarkably unfussy plant and will tolerate most
garden sites, but given a choice, it would prefer sun or light shade
(where it will flower slightly better) in fertile, well-drained soil.
Prune after flowering by cutting back the flowered stems to a
healthy new bud. This is also the time to renovate congested plants
by reducing the bush by a quarter.

PLANT PROFILE

HEIGHT 10ft (3m)

SPREAD 10ft (3m)

SITE Full sun or light shade

SOIL Fertile, free-draining

HARDINESS Z6–9 H9–6

FLOWERING Winter and
early spring

J | *Jasminum officinale* Common jasmine

THE TWINING STEMS of this fabulously scented deciduous or semievergreen climber can be grown over a pergola, trellis, or arch. It needs a sheltered, sunny position for three reasons: first, it needs protection from frost; second, while it tolerates shade, it flowers best in full sun; and third, the scent from its white flowers will linger in an enclosed space. When planting, allow plenty of room for its rampant growth. Prune only to remove frost-damaged growth, or, after flowering, to thin out congested stems.

OTHER VARIETIES *J. beesianum* (shorter-growing, pinkish red flowers); *J. officinale* 'Argenteovariegatum' (white-margined, gray-green leaves); *J. officinale* 'Aureovariegatum' (leaves marked with yellow).

PLANT PROFILE
HEIGHT 40ft (12m)
SITE Full sun
SOIL Light, free-draining
HARDINESS Z8–11 H12–8
FLOWERING Summer to early autumn

Kalmia latifolia Calico bush

K

A DENSELY GROWING EVERGREEN, the calico bush is awash in pink (sometimes white) flowers in the first half of summer. Grow this beautiful shrub as a hedge or as an individual specimen plant on acidic soils. It is also suitable for planting on the fringes of a woodland garden. In the second half of summer, after flowering is over, the glossy, dark green leaves make a good backdrop for late-summer shrubs. Indulge its preference for moist, rich soil by adding a really thick mulch of garden compost over the root area in spring.

OTHER VARIETIES *K. latifolia* 'Freckles' (pink flowers with dark spots); *K. latifolia* 'Shooting Star' (white flowers); *K. latifolia* 'Silver Dollar' (white flowers).

PLANT PROFILE
HEIGHT 10ft (3m)
SPREAD 10ft (3m)
SITE Sun or partial shade
SOIL Acidic, moist, fertile
HARDINESS Z5–9 H9–5
FLOWERING Late spring to midsummer

K | *Kerria japonica* 'Pleniflora'

WHEN PLANTING KERRIA, make allowances for its vigorous, suckering habit. 'Pleniflora' will spread to 10ft (3m) in time, producing masses of vertical, thin, twiggy stems that bear long-lasting, pomponlike double flowers. Its generous proportions mean that it is best grown as part of a perimeter hedge, in a large border, or in a woodland garden. After flowering, the bright green leaves are the main feature until they fall in autumn. All kerria needs is free-draining soil in sun or light shade. Cutting flowered stems back to different levels will produce blooms at different heights the following year.

OTHER VARIETIES *K. japonica* 'Golden Guinea' (single yellow flowers); *K. japonica* 'Picta' (smaller, cream-margined gray-green leaves).

PLANT PROFILE

HEIGHT 10ft (3m)

SPREAD 10ft (3m)

SITE Full sun or partial shade

SOIL Fertile, free-draining

HARDINESS Z5–9 H8–3

FLOWERING Mid- and late spring

Kolkwitzia amabilis 'Pink Cloud' Beauty bush

K

THE COMMON NAME OF THIS PLANT is completely justified because every arching stem on this dense, deciduous, twiggy shrub becomes laden with deep pink flowers, each with a yellow throat. It is a remarkable sight at the end of spring, before the summer garden gets into full swing. Start out right and give it a large space to grow into—it would be criminal to have to cut it back to keep it contained. Fertile, well-drained soil and plenty of summer sun are all the goodies it requires. Thin out the stems after flowering by cutting back to a strong bud, to help maintain vigor.

OTHER VARIETY *K. amabilis* (lighter pink flowers).

PLANT PROFILE

HEIGHT 10ft (3m)

SPREAD 12ft (4m)

SITE Full sun

SOIL Fertile, free-draining

HARDINESS Z6–9 H9–1

FLOWERING Late spring and early summer

Lapageria rosea Chilean bellflower

THE NATIONAL FLOWER OF CHILE, *Lapageria rosea* is a well-behaved evergreen climber that thrives on slightly acidic soils. It is an impressive plant with long-lasting, bell-shaped, waxy flowers that appear from midsummer onward. The twining stems of dark green leaves need a slightly shady wall with horizontal wires to hang on to, or a pergola to climb over. In colder areas it will need the shelter of a warm wall and protection from wind. Pruning should be kept to a minimum, but it's fine to remove crowded or damaged growth after flowering.

OTHER VARIETIES *L. rosea* var. *albiflora* (white flowers); *L. rosea* 'Nash Court' (soft pink flowers with darker pink mottling).

PLANT PROFILE
HEIGHT 15ft (5m)
SITE Partial shade
SOIL Slightly acidic, fertile, moist but free-draining
HARDINESS Z10–11 H12–10
FLOWERING Midsummer to late autumn

Lathyrus latifolius Everlasting pea

L

NOT TO BE CONFUSED with the highly scented *Lathyrus odoratus* (sweet pea), the everlasting pea is a cottage-garden beauty that produces prolific clusters of rich pink flowers. Cut the topgrowth back to ground level in spring to encourage new shoots, and train it to grow up a wigwam of bamboo canes—wrap the structure in wire so that the tendrils have something to cling to. It can also be grown next to and encouraged to spread over shrubs, or teamed with the white flowers of 'White Pearl' for an eye-catching display. Water well in dry spells, and keep pinching out the growing tips to encourage bushiness. Regular deadheading will boost flowering.

OTHER VARIETY *L. vernus* (smaller-growing, purplish blue flowers).

PLANT PROFILE
HEIGHT 6ft (2m) or more
SPREAD 3ft (1m)
SITE Full sun or light shade
SOIL Fertile, free-draining
HARDINESS Z5–9 H9–5
FLOWERING Summer to early autumn

L *Laurus nobilis* Bay laurel

MORE FAMILIARLY KNOWN AS THE BAY TREE, this laurel rarely becomes a tree outside the Mediterranean. In colder, wetter regions it is typically sold as a stylish standard, with a bare trunk about 4ft (1.2m) high, topped by a ball of evergreen aromatic leaves that can be snipped for use in the kitchen. In spring, small greenish yellow flowers appear, followed on female plants by black berries. Plants grown in the border need to be sheltered from cold, drying winds that will damage the foliage, while potgrown plants should be brought under cover in winter. In mild city gardens, and by the sea, it can be grown as a neat hedge. Clip to shape in summer.

OTHER VARIETY *L. nobilis* 'Aurea' (golden yellow leaves).

PLANT PROFILE
HEIGHT 40ft (12m)
SPREAD 30ft (10m)
SITE Full sun or partial shade
SOIL Fertile, moist but free-draining
HARDINESS Z8–11 H12–1
FLOWERING Spring

Lavandula angustifolia 'Hidcote' Lavender

L

MORE THAN JUST A SCENTED SHRUB, lavender adds shape and form
to the garden. It is also a valuable food source for bees and many
butterflies. Dark purple-flowering 'Hidcote' is neatly compact and
makes a lovely edging plant for the front of a border or along a
path. When cut and dried, the pungent oils in the flowers make a
fragrant base for potpourri. To grow well, free-draining soil and full
sun are essential. Clip it in spring, but don't cut into the old wood.

OTHER VARIETIES *L. angustifolia* 'Munstead' (shorter, blue-purple
flowers); *L. angustifolia* 'Nana Alba' (shorter, white flowers); *L. angustifolia*
'Twickel Purple' (purple flowers).

PLANT PROFILE	
HEIGHT 24in (60cm)	
SPREAD 30in (75cm)	
SITE Full sun	
SOIL Free-draining	
HARDINESS Z5–8 H8–3	
FLOWERING Mid- and late summer	

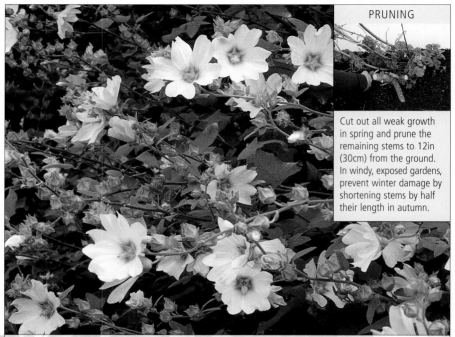

PRUNING

Cut out all weak growth in spring and prune the remaining stems to 12in (30cm) from the ground. In windy, exposed gardens, prevent winter damage by shortening stems by half their length in autumn.

Lavatera 'Barnsley' Tree mallow

A QUICK-GROWING SEMIEVERGREEN, 'Barnsley' thickens up in early summer with dozens of arching stems and then produces masses of delicate red-eyed white flowers. Get it off to a good start with very free-draining soil and plenty of sun. It will also welcome the support and shelter of a sunny wall or fence. Lavateras are not long-lived and after six or so years need replacing; alternatively, take cuttings in early summer to provide new plants. In winter, brush off heavy snow before it snaps the branches, and in spring, cut back frost-damaged stems.

OTHER VARIETIES *L. assurgentiflora* (cerise flowers); *L.* 'Bredon Springs' (mauvish flowers); *L.* 'Burgundy Wine' (dark-veined pink flowers).

PLANT PROFILE

HEIGHT 6ft (2m)

SPREAD 6ft (2m)

SITE Full sun

SOIL Light to average, free-draining

HARDINESS Z7–9 H9–7

FLOWERING Summer

Ledum groenlandicum Labrador tea

L

IF YOU ARE LOOKING FOR A USEFUL, upright, evergreen shrub for the border or heather garden, then consider Labrador tea. There's no need to worry about its hardiness, since it is a native of some pretty chilly places—Greenland, Alaska, and Canada—and is named after the Canadian Atlantic coastal region. It produces sprays of white flowers from late spring, and needs rich, moist but well-drained soil that is acidic to neutral. Pruning is not usually necessary, but an all-over trim after flowering will keep it looking neat.

OTHER VARIETY *L. palustre* (variable height, white spring flowers).

PLANT PROFILE
HEIGHT 3ft (1m)
SPREAD 4ft (1.2m)
SITE Full sun or partial shade
SOIL Preferably acidic, moist, fertile, free-draining
HARDINESS Z2–6 H6–1
FLOWERING Late spring

L | *Leonotis leonurus* Lion's ear

FEATURING STRONG SHADES OF RED AND ORANGE, lion's ear is a good choice for a late-season, brightly colored border. Deciduous or semievergreen, this South African shrub features an attractive mix of foliage and flowers. The leaves are thin and needlelike, up to about 5in (12cm) long, and the flower clusters appear in tiers up the tall stems from autumn to winter. A very tender plant, it needs a mild, sheltered, sunny garden site with free-draining soil to survive over winter. Play it safe and pot it in late autumn so you'll be able to bring it into the warmth of a conservatory for the winter. Once flowering is over, prune lightly in spring to maintain shape, if necessary.

PLANT PROFILE
HEIGHT 6ft (2m)
SPREAD 3ft (1m)
SITE Full sun
SOIL Free-draining
HARDINESS Z12–15 H12–6
FLOWERING Autumn to early winter

Leptospermum scoparium 'Red Damask' New Zealand tea tree   L

ALTHOUGH CALLED A TREE, 'Red Damask' is actually a medium-sized evergreen shrub. It has small, aromatic leaves and, at the start of summer, is covered in small, dark red flowers. Give it a very light all-over trim after flowering to increase bushiness and flowering. It requires free-draining, moderately fertile soil and a sunny, sheltered, frost-free site is essential. If 'Red Damask' grows successfully in your garden, try some of the other attractive forms, especially the 16ft-(5m-) tall *Leptospermum lanigerum*.

OTHER VARIETIES *L. scoparium* 'Nichollsii' (crimson flowers, purple-tinged leaves); *L. scoparium* 'Snow Flurry' (double white flowers).

PLANT PROFILE

HEIGHT 10ft (3m)

SPREAD 10ft (3m)

SITE Full sun or partial shade

SOIL Average, free-draining

HARDINESS Z12–15 H12–10

FLOWERING Late spring and early summer

L

Lespedeza thunbergii Bush clover

CONSIDERING THAT IT IS AMONG THE VERY BEST of the hardy
flowering autumn shrubs, it's surprising that *Lespedeza thunbergii* isn't
more widely grown. It is slow to get going, not developing leaves
until the early summer, but the arching, spreading stems produce a
pleasant, relaxed feel. The autumn show consists of airy sprays of
small, striking, purple-pink flowers. It tends to be cut back in cold
winters but reliably puts out new growth the following spring.
Because it develops later than other plants, you may think it has
died, but don't give up on it too quickly. Ideally, bush clover likes
average, free-draining soil, but it should also survive on heavier clay.

OTHER VARIETY *L. bicolor* (purple-pink flowers, dark green leaves).

PLANT PROFILE
HEIGHT 6ft (2m)
SPREAD 10ft (3m)
SITE Full sun
SOIL Average, light, free-draining
HARDINESS Z6–8 H8–6
FLOWERING Early autumn

Leucothoe fontanesiana 'Rainbow' Highland doghobble

L

FOR GOOD GROUND COVER ON ACIDIC SOIL, you can't do much better than this eye-catching evergreen shrub. It is upright with arching stems and leathery cream, green, and pink mottled leaves that redden up in autumn. In late spring, tiny white flowers appear in dangling clusters. A shady wooded area of the garden, with its rich, reliably moist soil, is an ideal spot. In early spring, cut away any crossing or badly placed stems to improve the overall shape.

OTHER VARIETIES *L. fontanesiana* (larger-growing, white flowers); *L. fontanesiana* 'Rollissonii' (narrow lance-shaped leaves); *L.* 'Zeblid' (red-purple young leaves, turning bronze in autumn).

PLANT PROFILE
HEIGHT 5ft (1.5m)
SPREAD 6ft (2m)
SITE Deep or partial shade
SOIL Acid, moist, fertile
HARDINESS Z5–8 H8–5
FLOWERING Late spring

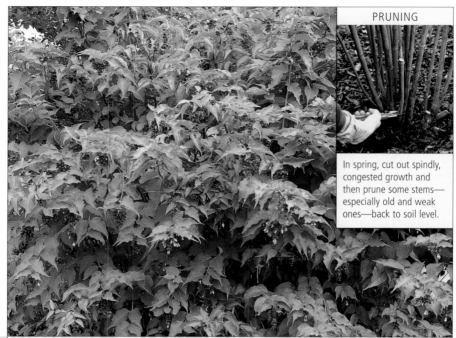

PRUNING

In spring, cut out spindly, congested growth and then prune some stems— especially old and weak ones—back to soil level.

L

Leycesteria formosa Himalayan honeysuckle

IN SUMMER, THE HIMALAYAN HONEYSUCKLE is a solid thicket of bamboolike leafy growth and dangling flower stems of unusual richly colored bracts that hold the small white blooms. The flowers are then followed by dark purple berries that last well into autumn. In winter, although it is deciduous, its green stems are striking enough to maintain interest. A free-draining, moderately fertile soil and a sheltered position out of the wind suit it best. Be warned that unless you weed thoroughly around the base of the plant, you will end up with dozens of quick-rooting seedlings. Each spring, prune several stems to the ground to force up fresh, new, leafy growth.

OTHER VARIETY *L. crocothyrsos* (golden yellow flowers, green berries).

PLANT PROFILE
HEIGHT 6ft (2m)
SPREAD 6ft (2m)
SITE Full sun or partial shade
SOIL Average, free-draining
HARDINESS Z7–9 H9–6
FLOWERING Summer to early autumn

Ligustrum ovalifolium 'Aureum' Golden privet

L

DON'T DISMISS PRIVETS AS BEING DULL—many make first-rate shrubs, with strong, dense, evergreen foliage and strongly scented flowers that are followed by tiny, glossy, black berries. 'Aureum' has broad yellow leaf markings ('Argenteum' is similar with white markings) and can be grown in all types of soil, from rich to poor. Note that when grown in poor soil on an exposed site, it can become semievergreen. Prune in early spring to remove poorly placed stems. If you wish to treat it as a low-growing hedge, it will withstand severe pruning in early and late summer. For the best leaf color, grow in full sun.

OTHER VARIETIES *L. obtusifolium* (dark green leaves, later purple-tinged); *L. quihoui* (taller, mid-green leaves); *L.* 'Vicaryi' (yellow leaves).

PLANT PROFILE
HEIGHT 12ft (4m)
SPREAD 12ft (4m)
SITE Full sun or partial shade
SOIL Average, free-draining
HARDINESS Z6–10 H10–9
FLOWERING Midsummer

L | *Lindera obtusiloba* Japanese spicebush

IDEALLY SUITED TO A WOODLAND GARDEN, *Lindera obtusiloba* makes
a large shrub or a small tree. For the best results it must have moist
but free-draining, acidic soil and light shade. Provided these
conditions are met, you will be rewarded with a magnificent
deciduous shrub with aromatic, glossy, dark green leaves that turn
mustard yellow in autumn. Dark yellow, star-shaped flowers appear
in early spring and are followed on female plants—if there is a male
plant nearby for pollination—by glossy red-brown berries.

OTHER VARIETY *L. benzoin* (smaller-growing, aromatic bright green
leaves, yellow in autumn, greenish yellow flowers followed by red berries
on female plants).

PLANT PROFILE
HEIGHT 20ft (6m)
SPREAD 20ft (6m)
SITE Partial shade
SOIL Acidic, fertile, moist but free-draining
HARDINESS Z6–9 H9–6
FLOWERING Early and midspring

Lithodora diffusa 'Heavenly Blue'

L

LOW-GROWING PLANTS need careful positioning, and one as beautiful as 'Heavenly Blue' should go right at the front of a border, beside a path, or in a rock garden or raised bed where it can be seen clearly. Rarely growing more than ankle-high, its energies are put into spreading sideways, and from the end of spring it becomes a carpet of azure blue flowers. It is a lover of acidic soil—which is easy enough to provide in a self-contained raised bed—and good drainage, boosted by digging in plenty of horticultural sand. For an effective contrast, grow blue- and white-flowering types together.

OTHER VARIETIES *L. diffusa* 'Alba' (white flowers); *L. rosmarinifolia* (taller, gentian blue flowers); *L. zahnii* (taller, blue or white flowers).

PLANT PROFILE
HEIGHT 6in (15cm)
SPREAD 24in (60cm)
SITE Full sun
SOIL Acidic, fertile, free-draining
HARDINESS Z6–8 H8–6
FLOWERING Late spring and summer

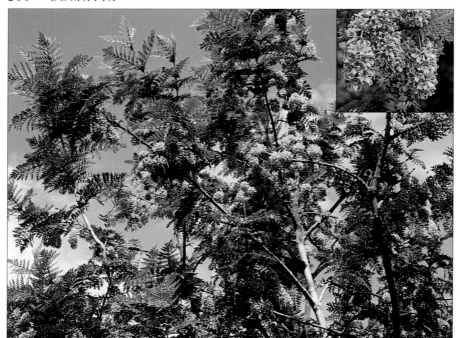

L | *Lomatia ferruginea* Palmilla

FOR SITES WITH POOR, ACIDIC SOIL, there are precious few evergreen, architectural, bushy shrubs or small trees from which to choose, but this is one of the best. The spindly, fernlike leaves with their fawn underfelting will add a touch of exotica to the garden, and, in midsummer, the branches are hung with large swags of yellow and red star-shaped flowers. It needs shelter from winter weather, especially cold, drying winds, and is best sited beside a warm sunny wall or in a wooded area of the garden or shrub border, where it is surrounded by other plants.

OTHER VARIETY *L. tinctoria* (shorter-growing, fragrant, creamy white flowers).

PLANT PROFILE
HEIGHT 30ft (10m)
SPREAD 15ft (5m)
SITE Full sun or partial shade
SOIL Acidic, moist but free-draining
HARDINESS Z11 H12–8
FLOWERING Midsummer

Lonicera fragrantissima Honeysuckle

FORGET THE SUMMER-FLOWERING CLIMBERS—this is a deciduous or semievergreen shrub that blooms from the end of winter into spring, filling the garden with its rich fragrance. Given the lack of winter-scented plants, this one is extremely valuable. For the best show of flowers, grow it against a sunny, sheltered wall in rich, moist but well-drained soil. After flowering, prune back the flowered stems to a strong bud, and encourage vigorous new growth on established plants by cutting one in four of the old stems to the ground.

OTHER VARIETIES *L. involucrata* (dark yellow flowers tinged red); *L. korolkowii* (larger-growing, rose pink flowers).

PLANT PROFILE
HEIGHT 6ft (2m)
SPREAD 10ft (3m)
SITE Full sun or partial shade
SOIL Fertile, moist but free-draining
HARDINESS Z4–8 H8–3
FLOWERING Winter and early spring

L *Lonicera japonica* 'Halliana' Japanese honeysuckle

THIS FAST-GROWING, QUICK-SPREADING evergreen or semievergreen climber guarantees masses of leafy growth and pure white, richly scented flowers. The flowers later turn yellow and are followed by tiny black berries. An extremely vigorous grower, it needs a large expanse of wall or a sturdy tree, pergola, or shed to sprawl over. A typical honeysuckle, it prefers rich, moist but well-drained soil with shade at the base of the stem. If it outgrows its allotted space, cut back long stems in early spring to a healthy bud.

OTHER VARIETY *L. japonica* var. *repens* (purple-tinged foliage, white flowers are flushed red-purple).

PLANT PROFILE

HEIGHT 30ft (10m)

SITE Full sun or partial shade

SOIL Fertile, moist but free-draining

HARDINESS Z4–11 H12–1

FLOWERING Spring to late summer

Lonicera nitida 'Baggesen's Gold' Honeysuckle

THE GREAT ATTRACTION of this dense, bushy evergreen shrub lies in its yellow leaves. Make a feature of them by pruning its mass of stems into shapely topiary, or use it like boxwood (*Buxus*) as a mini-hedge for parterres and knot gardens. If left unpruned, white spring flowers are followed by tiny, blue-purple berries. To keep it neat, it needs trimming at least three times a year between spring and autumn. Any free-draining, fertile soil is suitable.

OTHER VARIETIES *L. involucrata* (smaller-growing, red-tinged dark yellow flowers); *L. nitida* (creamy white flowers, blue-purple berries); *L. x purpusii* 'Winter Beauty' (smaller-growing, white and yellow flowers).

PLANT PROFILE
HEIGHT 11ft (3.5m)
SPREAD 10ft (3m)
SITE Full sun or partial shade
SOIL Fertile, free-draining
HARDINESS Z6–9 H9–6
FLOWERING Spring

L

Lonicera periclymenum 'Serotina' Late Dutch honeysuckle

ALSO KNOWN AS WOODBINE, this honeysuckle comes from the deciduous form found in hedges and trees in the countryside. The flowers have dark red-purple markings and are noted for their strong evening scent. If space permits, also grow 'Belgica' (the early Dutch honeysuckle) with its red-streaked white flowers that open earlier in the season. Both like rich, moist but well-drained soil with shade at the base of the stem. When established, prune shoots back by one-third after flowering to keep it within bounds.

OTHER VARIETIES *L.* x *americana* (fragrant yellow flowers flushed red-purple); *L. etrusca* 'Superba' (smaller-growing, cream flowers turning orange); *L.* x *heckrottii* (flowers pink outside, yellow-orange inside).

PLANT PROFILE

HEIGHT 22ft (7m)

SITE Full sun or partial shade

SOIL Fertile, moist but free-draining

HARDINESS Z5–9 H9–5

FLOWERING Mid- and late summer

Lonicera x *tellmanniana* Honeysuckle

THIS CLIMBER IS SLIGHTLY DIFFERENT from some of the more rampant, vigorous honeysuckles because its deciduous growth is quite modest. Although they carry no fragrance, the flowers are such an attractive dark orange that they are worth growing for their color alone. For the best show of flowers, plant it in light shade—although it also grows well in full sun—in cool, moist, free-draining soil. Prune established plants back by up to one-third to strong, young growth immediately after flowering.

OTHER VARIETIES *L. periclymenum* 'Belgica' (red-streaked white flowers, turning yellow); *L. tragophylla* (red-tinted, yellow or orange-yellow flowers).

PLANT PROFILE

HEIGHT 15ft (5m)

SITE Full sun or partial shade

SOIL Fertile, cool, moist but free-draining

HARDINESS Z7–9 H9–7

FLOWERING Late spring to midsummer

L *Lupinus arboreus* Californian tree lupin

FOR THE MORE INFORMAL STYLE OF GARDEN, the Californian tree lupin makes an impressive, fast-growing, semievergreen shrub. It produces a rather sprawling mound of stems tipped by candlelike flowering spikes, each up to 12in (30cm) long. It requires quite specific conditions to do well, with light and sandy, quick-draining, reasonably fertile soil, and the type of mild, coastal, frost-free climate you'd typically find in California. An established tree lupin will provide useful shelter for other plants that dislike being buffeted by strong winds. Unfortunately, it is short-lived, so after three or four years, it's worth taking cuttings to grow new plants to replace the parent plant, or allow it to self-seed and move the seedlings to where they are needed.

PLANT PROFILE
HEIGHT 6ft (2m)
SPREAD 6ft (2m)
SITE Full sun
SOIL Fertile, free-draining
HARDINESS Z9–10 H10–9
FLOWERING Late spring and summer

Lycium barbarum Wolfberry

NO MATTER HOW POOR YOUR SOIL, this quick-growing, often spiny, deciduous shrub will still shoot up to make a substantial hedge that will help protect a coastal garden from strong winds. Dry slopes are another suitable site. Due to its scrambling and arching habit, it is not the neatest of shrubs, but you can keep it in shape by pruning it immediately after flowering. If you are growing it as a hedge, give it a hard prune in spring. Small clusters of purple to pink flowers appear in late spring and summer; the subsequent orange-red or yellow berries are glossy and small.

PLANT PROFILE

HEIGHT 11ft (3.5m) or more

SPREAD 15ft (5m)

SITE Full sun

SOIL Average, free-draining

HARDINESS Z6–9 H9–5

FLOWERING Late spring and summer

M | *Magnolia stellata* Star magnolia

ALTHOUGH SOME MAGNOLIAS make deciduous trees up to 10m (30ft) high, the star magnolia is a more manageable shrub. The unusual flowers, which open from blush pink buds on bare stems, look like white spiders up to 5in (12cm) across. If the flowers are damaged by frost, more will appear. This is one of the best feature plants around, but it isn't scented (although if that's what you're after, there is a big choice of magnolias). The soil should be rich, moist but well drained, and preferably acidic, although it will tolerate the slightly alkaline. Prune for shape when young, then only to remove dead wood.

OTHER VARIETIES *M.* 'Betty' (cup-shaped, purple-red flowers, white insides); *M. globosa* (taller-growing, white flowers with red centers).

PLANT PROFILE
HEIGHT 10ft (3m)
SPREAD 12ft (4m)
SITE Full sun
SOIL Fertile, moist but free-draining
HARDINESS Z5–9 H9–5
FLOWERING Early and midspring

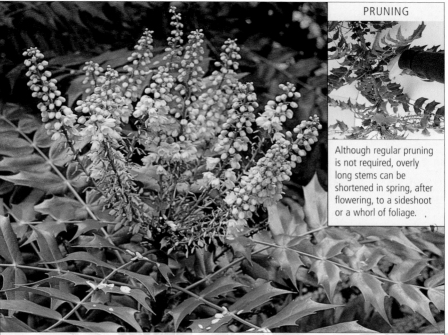

Although regular pruning is not required, overly long stems can be shortened in spring, after flowering, to a sideshoot or a whorl of foliage.

Mahonia x *media* 'Charity' Holly grape

M

ONE GLANCE AT 'CHARITY' and it's easy to see why it has become so popular. A superb architectural plant with outward-pointing, dark evergreen, spiny leaves, it also produces dozens of long spikes of scented, yellow, winter flowers. Such a strong, tough, upright plant makes a highly attractive, impenetrable hedge. In general, mahonias prefer full or partial shade, but they will tolerate direct sunlight as long as the soil is not too dry. In the late afternoon winter sun, the flowers look stunning. Prune only for shape after flowering.

OTHER VARIETIES *M.* x *media* 'Arthur Menzies' (lemon yellow flowers); *M.* x *media* 'Buckland' (bright yellow flowers); *M.* x *media* 'Winter Sun' (densely clustered bright yellow flowers).

PLANT PROFILE
HEIGHT 15ft (5m)
SPREAD 12ft (4m)
SITE Full or partial shade
SOIL Fertile, moist but free-draining
HARDINESS Z8–9 H9–8
FLOWERING Late autumn to late winter

BRACKET FUNGUS

Crabapples are prone to this fungus, which attacks most often in the autumn. Removing the bracts from the base of the shrub may slow its spread, but deterioration often continues inside the plant.

M *Malus toringo* subsp. *sargentii* Crabapple

UNLIKE MOST CRABAPPLES, which are deciduous trees, this is more like a spreading shrub, being slightly wider than it is tall. Wild gardens will suit it best, or, perhaps, the perimeters of a more formal garden. It isn't stretching the truth to say that it is sensational when in flower: the tightly furled, fat pink buds cover the stems and open to beautiful white blooms. These are followed by long-lasting, dark red fruits that decorate the branches from midsummer. It is not fussy about soil conditions and will even tolerate a site in light shade.

PLANT PROFILE

HEIGHT 12ft (4m)

SPREAD 15ft (5m)

SITE Full sun or light shade

SOIL Average, moist but free-draining

HARDINESS Z4–8 H8–1

FLOWERING Late spring

Menziesia ciliicalyx var. *purpurea*

M

GIVEN ACIDIC SOIL, this slow-growing, deciduous shrub is easy to please and will produce an attractive covering of small, dark purple-pink, urn-shaped flowers at the end of spring. Its compact size makes it perfect for the shady end of a border or a small woodland garden. One important thing to do at planting time is to incorporate plenty of organic matter into and around the planting hole, because it must have moist, rich soil to do well. Throw in partial shade and shelter from cold winds and you're on to a winner.

OTHER VARIETY *M. ferruginea* (larger-growing, red-flushed yellow flowers, mid-green leaves turn red in autumn).

PLANT PROFILE
HEIGHT 3ft (1m)
SPREAD 3ft (1m)
SITE Partial shade
SOIL Acidic, fertile, moist but free-draining
HARDINESS Z6–9 H9–7
FLOWERING Late spring and early summer

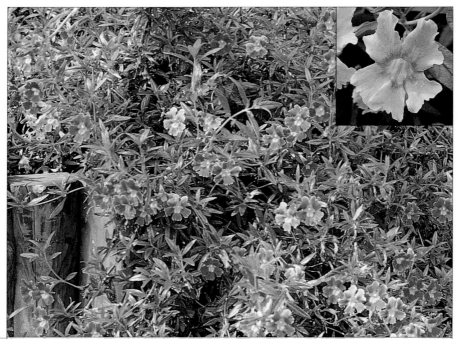

M | *Mimulus aurantiacus* Monkey flower

MULTIBRANCHING AT THE BASE, with vertical stems, the monkey flower puts on a lavish, continuous show of blooms. In a range of strong oranges, yellows, and dark reds, they are open, trumpet-shaped and nearly 2in (5cm) long with wavy edges (*see inset*). The soil is the most crucial factor and must be free-draining and rich; when this is coupled with a mild, sunny position, flowers will be produced from late summer to autumn. Plants are often short-lived, but by taking cuttings in early summer you can guarantee replacements.

OTHER VARIETIES *M. aurantiacus* var. *puniceus* (taller, brick red to orange flowers, needs mild conditions); *M. longiflorus* (dark red, orange, lemon yellow, or cream flowers with orange bands).

PLANT PROFILE	
HEIGHT 3ft (1m)	
SPREAD 3ft (1m)	
SITE Full sun	
SOIL Fertile, free-draining	
HARDINESS Z7–11 H12–7	
FLOWERING Late summer to autumn	

Mitraria coccinea Botellita

GIVEN THE RIGHT CONDITIONS, this scrambling South American evergreen shrub will put on a long-lasting show of glossy, dark green leaves and the richest red flowers. The buds start to open at the end of spring, with flowering continuing through into early autumn. It's quite a fussy plant—although well worth the effort— needing a cool, mild, sheltered site on rich, acidic soil that's moist but free-draining. Ideally the roots should be in light shade and the top of the plant in sun. A wooded area or a partially shaded border is ideal. Lightly prune for shape in mid- to late spring.

PLANT PROFILE

HEIGHT 6ft (2m)

SITE Light shade

SOIL Acidic, fertile, moist but free-draining

HARDINESS Z10–11 H12–10

FLOWERING Late spring to autumn

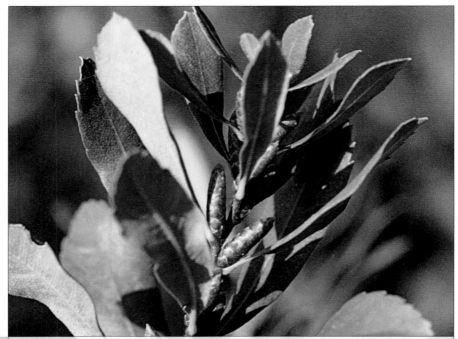

M | *Myrica gale* Bog myrtle

WATERLOGGED, ACIDIC SOIL…impossible conditions for most garden plants but perfect for bog myrtle. From midspring, this deciduous, thicket-forming shrub bears clusters of reddish catkins among its long, dark green leaves. Plant it in groups along a well-used route through the garden, perhaps beside a wooded area. Having the plants close by means you can just reach out and crush a few of the leaves to enjoy their sweet aroma. *Myrica cerifera* (wax myrtle) grows three times as high as *M. gale* and, although it is not quite as hardy, it can be evergreen in mild regions.

PLANT PROFILE	
HEIGHT 5ft (1.5m)	
SPREAD 5ft (1.5m)	
SITE Sun	
SOIL Wet, fertile	
HARDINESS Z1–6	
FLOWERING Mid- and late spring	

Myrtus communis subsp. *tarentina* Common myrtle

BEING ONLY ABOUT HALF THE HEIGHT of its parent, *Myrtus communis*, this variety is a more manageable size and compact enough for most gardens. The evergreen leaves are aromatic when crushed, and the pinkish-white flowers, and subsequent tiny white berries, put on a good show in mild and sheltered Mediterranean-style or courtyard gardens. Coming from a warm climate, it needs excellent drainage, plenty of sun, and protection from cold, drying winds. The longer and hotter the summer, the better the display of flowers will be.

OTHER VARIETIES *M. communis* subsp. *tarentina* 'Microphylla Variegata' (white-margined leaves); *M. lechleriana* (taller-growing, fragrant white flowers, aromatic red berries ripening to black).

PLANT PROFILE
HEIGHT 5ft (1.5m)
SPREAD 5ft (1.5m)
SITE Full sun
SOIL Moist but free-draining
HARDINESS Z8–9 H9–8
FLOWERING Mid- to late summer or early autumn

N | *Nandina domestica* Heavenly bamboo

THE WORD "BAMBOO" in this plant's common name is a misnomer— it's an evergreen or semievergreen shrub with bamboolike stems and elegant foliage. The divided leaves are reddish purple when young, maturing to green, then reverting to red again in late autumn (*see inset*). In midsummer, clusters of small, star-shaped flowers with yellow centers appear; in a warm season, they are followed by bright red berries. A sunny, sheltered site is essential, with moist but free-draining soil. If the winter is very cold, there is a risk it may not survive. Clip lightly for shape in midspring.

OTHER VARIETY *N. domestica* 'Fire Power' (smaller-growing, bright red leaves).

PLANT PROFILE
HEIGHT 6ft (2m)
SPREAD 5ft (1.5m)
SITE Full sun
SOIL Moist but free-draining
HARDINESS Z6–11 H12–4
FLOWERING Midsummer

Neillia thibetica

IN EARLY SUMMER, the gracefully zigzagging branches of this thicket–forming shrub hold clusters of small, rose pink, tubular flowers (*see inset*) which, coupled with the bright green, lobed leaves, make a lasting impression. Such a broad spread makes it an unsuitable choice for a small urban garden but perfect for a woodland setting or a large shrub border. After flowering is finished, give it a light clip for shape. To renovate an established plant, cut one in four of the old flowered stems down to the ground to encourage new growth. Remove suckers in the autumn.

OTHER VARIETY *N. sinensis* (tubular, pinkish white flowers, attractively jagged leaves).

PLANT PROFILE

HEIGHT 6ft (2m)

SPREAD 6ft (2m)

SITE Full sun or partial shade

SOIL Fertile, free-draining

HARDINESS Z6–9 H9–6

FLOWERING Early summer

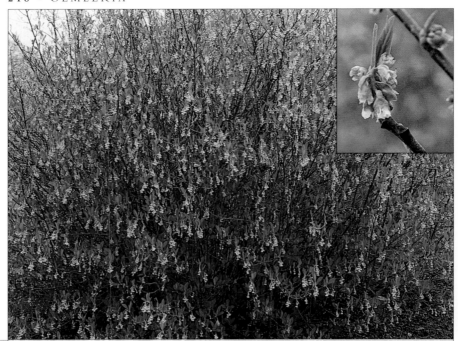

O · *Oemleria cerasiformis* Indian plum

IF YOU HAVE ROOM IN YOUR GARDEN, be sure to include a female and male Indian plum from the western states of North America. The female shrub carries the distinctive small, black, plumlike fruit, while the male produces a better display of flowers. Both make a very dense thicket of upright growth that tends to arch toward the top. Stems are thickly covered in glossy, dark green leaves, while the clusters of small, white, bell-shaped flowers (*see inset*) are faintly almond-scented. Another bonus is that, despite being deciduous, the Indian plum is one of the first plants to come into leaf in late winter. After flowering, cut back flowered shoots to strong new buds.

PLANT PROFILE

HEIGHT 8ft (2.5m) or more

SPREAD 12ft (4m)

SITE Sun or partial shade

SOIL Fertile, moist but free-draining

HARDINESS Z6–10 H10–6

FLOWERING Early spring

Olearia x *haastii* Daisy bush

THE APTLY NAMED DAISY BUSH really does produce a profusion of white, daisylike flowers in summer. It is mostly grown in coastal gardens, where it forms a salt-tolerant, sheltering, evergreen hedge. Prune it to shape as often as you wish because it will quickly throw up new growth. The 10ft- (3m-) high *Olearia avicenniifolia* and the 6ft- (2m-) high *O. nummulariifolia* (both scented) are also suitable for mild areas. All need excellent drainage, though they are not fussy about soil.

OTHER VARIETIES *O. cheesemanii* (taller-growing, yellow-centered white flowers); *O.* 'Henry Travers' (lilac and purple flowers); *O. solandri* (very fragrant, pale yellow flowers).

PLANT PROFILE
HEIGHT 6ft (2m)
SPREAD 10ft (3m)
SITE Full sun
SOIL Average, free-draining
HARDINESS Z12–15 H12–10
FLOWERING Mid- and late summer

O

Origanum 'Kent Beauty' Oregano

THERE ARE MORE AROMATIC FORMS OF OREGANO than 'Kent Beauty'—such as the pungent perennial *Origanum vulgare*—but few are as attractive. Evergreen and shrubby, 'Kent Beauty' has trailing, ground-hugging stems that are well suited to rock gardens or the tops of stone walls, where its stems can trail prettily down. From the sunnier climes of the Mediterranean and southwest Asia, oreganos won't survive saturating winter moisture and instead must have free-draining, even stony, soil with average fertility.

OTHER VARIETIES *O. amanum* (bigger, pink flowers, green bracts turning purple-pink); *O. laevigatum* 'Herrenhausen' (taller-growing, purple-pink flowers); *O. rotundifolium* (pink flowers, lemon-green bracts).

PLANT PROFILE	
HEIGHT 4in (10cm)	
SPREAD 8in (20cm)	
SITE Full sun	
SOIL Average, free-draining	
HARDINESS Z5–8 H8–5	
FLOWERING Summer	

Osmanthus delavayi

O

THIS RICHLY SCENTED EVERGREEN SHRUB is equally useful as a border shrub or shapely hedge. It can even be clipped and styled as topiary, and the dark green leaves are beautifully glossy and leathery. Although the scented flowers are small, they appear in huge numbers; inedible, black, olivelike berries follow. Prune after flowering to keep the plant small or, at the other extreme, let it grow into a giant, white-flowering specimen. Give it a sunny, sheltered position on fertile, free-draining soil.

OTHER VARIETIES *O. x burkwoodii* (very fragrant white flowers, seldom produces fruit); *O. decorus* (larger leaves); *O. heterophyllus* (holly-like leaves); *O. heterophyllus* 'Gulftide' (smaller-growing, very spiny leaves).

PLANT PROFILE
HEIGHT 6–20ft (2–6m)
SPREAD 12ft (4m)
SITE Full sun or partial shade
SOIL Fertile, free-draining
HARDINESS Z7–9 H9–7
FLOWERING Mid- and late spring

O   *Ozothamnus rosmarinifolius* Sea rosemary

THE NAME OF THIS PLANT derives from the pungent, rosemary-like aroma of its leaves. It isn't a substitute for the herb, however. In cooler-climate gardens, it needs a sunny, sheltered position and a thick, protective mulch of compost to help it survive the winter. From early summer, the strongly scented white flowers open from dense clusters of red buds. To create a more open, shapely plant, after flowering thin out a few stems.

OTHER VARIETIES *O. coralloides* (smaller-growing, yellowish white flowers); *O. ledifolius* (smaller-growing, white flowers); *O. rosmarinifolius* 'Silver Jubilee' (silvery gray leaves).

PLANT PROFILE
HEIGHT 6–10ft (2–3m)
SPREAD 5ft (1.5m)
SITE Full sun
SOIL Average, free-draining
HARDINESS Z8–9 H9–8
FLOWERING Early summer

Paeonia delavayi var. *ludlowii* Tree peony

P

DECIDUOUS TREE PEONIES are an extraordinary sight and are on a much grander scale than their smaller perennial relatives. In spring, the stiff, vertical stems are covered in large, bright green leaves. The vivid yellow flowers, up to 5in (12cm) wide, open at the top of the stems. Other tree peonies are available, mainly in reds, purple-reds, maroons, salmon pinks, and white, the widest choice coming from cultivars of *Paeonia suffruticosa*. Prune only for shape if necessary after flowering. Rich, moist but free-draining soil is preferred, with shelter from cold winds an essential.

OTHER VARIETIES *P. delavayi* (rich, dark red flowers); *P. tenuifolia* (smaller-growing, deep red flowers); *P. veitchii* (white or pink flowers).

PLANT PROFILE	
HEIGHT 5ft (1.5m)	
SPREAD 5ft (1.5m)	
SITE Sun or partial shade	
SOIL Fertile, moist but free-draining	
HARDINESS Z3–8 H8–1	
FLOWERING Late spring	

P

Paliurus spina-christi Christ's thorn

CHRIST'S CROWN OF THORNS was reputedly fashioned from this striking, prickly shrub. The thorny shoots are vicious, and if you want to protect your boundaries, this would make even the most determined burglar think twice about vaulting over. It is easy to grow, given full sun and well-drained soil—avoid heavy clay—in a mild, sheltered garden, and will soon make an impenetrable hedge. Starlike yellow flowers appear in summer and are followed by curious, flat, woody, disk-shaped fruits, 1in (2.5cm) wide. In autumn, the dark green leaves turn yellow before falling.

PLANT PROFILE	
HEIGHT 12ft (4m)	
SPREAD 10ft (3m)	
SITE Full sun	
SOIL Average, free-draining	
HARDINESS Z7–9 H9–7	
FLOWERING Summer	

Parthenocissus quinquefolia Virginia creeper

P

A REAL POWERHOUSE OF A CLIMBER that will soon cover the walls of even a tall building. In autumn the leaves turn spectacular shades of red before falling (*see inset*). Self-clinging, it climbs by means of tiny suckers on the growing stems that latch on like limpets—bear in mind that, once in place, prying them off is impossible, so position your plant wisely. To cope with the weight of such a large plant, walls must be in good condition and trees should be large and mature. Stop growth 12in (30cm) below a roofline by cutting through the stems in spring.

OTHER VARIETIES *P. henryana* (shorter, white-veined green leaves); *P. tricuspidata* (taller, deeply toothed leaves turn brilliant red to purple).

PLANT PROFILE
HEIGHT 50ft (15m) or more
SITE Sun or shade
SOIL Fertile, free-draining
HARDINESS Z7–9 H9–1
FLOWERING Summer

P

Passiflora caerulea Blue passionflower

THE BLUE PASSIONFLOWER from South America is one of the most exciting garden climbers. The exotic-looking flowers, up to 4in (10cm) across, look as though they belong in the jungle. In sheltered gardens, flowering is prolific and may be followed, in hot summers, by orange-yellow, egg-shaped fruit. The quick-growing stems will spiral up a trellis, horizontal wires attached to a sunny wall, or a hedge. Although it is an evergreen, it will lose its leaves if the winters are cold and windy. Mulch with compost in winter to protect the roots, and cut stems back in early spring if you want to restrict its spread.

OTHER VARIETIES *P. caerulea* 'Constance Elliott' (all-white flowers); *P. incarnata* (shorter-growing, pale purple flowers).

PLANT PROFILE

HEIGHT 30ft (10m) or more

SITE Full sun or partial shade

SOIL Moist but free-draining

HARDINESS Z6–9 H9–6

FLOWERING Summer to autumn

Penstemon fruticosus Shrubby penstemon

P

ALTHOUGH MOST PENSTEMONS are semievergreen perennials, *Penstemon fruticosus* counts as a small, evergreen shrub that is suitable for the front of a border or a rock garden. It spreads horizontally across the soil, putting down roots as it goes, but there's no need for concern because it is easily controlled with pruners. Its lavender purple flowers are typically funnel-shaped, and, like all penstemons, it needs average, sharply drained soil in full sun.

OTHER VARIETIES *P. fruticosus* var. *scouleri* (deep purple flowers); *P. hirsutus* (taller, pale violet flowers); *P. isophyllus* (red to deep pink flowers); *P. pinifolius* (scarlet flowers); *P. rupicola* (shorter, deep red-pink flowers).

PLANT PROFILE
HEIGHT 16in (40cm)
SPREAD 16in (40cm)
SITE Full sun or partial shade
SOIL Average, very free-draining
HARDINESS Z4–9 H9–1
FLOWERING Late spring and early summer

P | *Perovskia* 'Blue Spire' Russian sage

PEROVSKIAS ARE EXTREMELY USEFUL plants because they flower at the end of summer. 'Blue Spire' catches the eye with its erect, multibranching flower stems that bear more than a passing resemblance to lavender. The whole effect is wonderfully light and airy due to its finely dissected leaves, which are the palest silver-gray. Although technically a shrub, it is best treated as a perennial and cut back to the lowest stems in spring to encourage vigorous new growth. It is not fussy and will grow successfully near the sea in average-to-dry, free-draining soil and also on alkaline ground.

OTHER VARIETY *P. atriplicifolia* (violet-blue flowers, deeply cut gray-green leaves).

PLANT PROFILE
HEIGHT 4ft (1.2m)
SPREAD 3ft (1m)
SITE Full sun
SOIL Average, free-draining
HARDINESS Z6–9 H9–6
FLOWERING Late summer and early autumn

GREENWOOD CUTTING

In late spring, cut a nonflowering shoot and reduce it to 3in (8cm) with a straight cut below a leaf joint. Remove lower leaves and insert the cutting into a container of rooting medium. Water with a fungicidal solution and place the container in a propagator. Once rooted, pot the cutting.

Philadelphus coronarius 'Aureus' Mock orange

P

IF YOU WANT A HIGHLY SCENTED, DECIDUOUS SHRUB for a hedge or border, this is it. The exquisitely scented, creamy white flowers of 'Aureus' open in midsummer on closely packed stems. The young leaves are golden yellow in spring and summer, later turning green. To avoid leaf burn, choose a site in dappled shade. Unlike most mock oranges, this one will tolerate dryish soil. After flowering, cut one in four of the stems to the ground to promote new, bushy growth. Greenwood cuttings can be taken in spring (*see inset*).

OTHER VARIETIES *P. coronarius* 'Variegatus' (white flowers, white-margined leaves); *P. microphyllus* (smaller-growing, white flowers).

PLANT PROFILE

HEIGHT 8ft (2.5m)

SPREAD 5ft (1.5m)

SITE Dappled shade

SOIL Average, free-draining

HARDINESS Z4–7 H7–1

FLOWERING Summer

P

Philadelphus 'Manteau d'Hermine' Mock orange

EVERY GARDEN NEEDS at least one richly scented, deciduous mock orange. Some are tall—'Beauclerk' hits 8ft (2.5m) in height—while others are spreading—'Belle Etoile' grows up to 8ft (2.5m) wide— but 'Manteau d'Hermine' is a more modest, wiry plant. It is not quite as richly scented as the first two, but the double flowers last slightly longer. Grow it in average, free-draining soil, and after flowering, remove one in four of the stems to encourage new growth.

OTHER VARIETIES *P.* 'Innocence' (taller, single or semidouble, fragrant white flowers, yellow-mottled leaves); *P.* 'Sybille' (fragrant white and purple flowers); *P.* 'Virginal' (taller, fragrant, double white flowers).

PLANT PROFILE
HEIGHT 30in (75cm)
SPREAD 5ft (1.5m)
SITE Full sun or partial shade
SOIL Average, free-draining
HARDINESS Z5–8 H8–5
FLOWERING Early and midsummer

Phlomis fruticosa Jerusalem sage

IN THE FREE-DRAINING SOIL of a Mediterranean or gravel garden, Jerusalem sage will survive low temperatures, but in colder climates with damper soil it will need the protection of a warm, sunny wall. The evergreen, 4in- (10cm-) long, gray-green leaves provide plenty of substance and contrast well with shrubs that have dark green foliage. From early summer, dark golden yellow flowers appear at the top of the stems. Clip in spring or after flowering for shape.

OTHER VARIETIES *P. chrysophylla* (golden yellow flowers); *P. italica* (lilac-pink flowers, woolly leaves); *P. purpurea* (purple to pink, sometimes white, flowers); *P. russeliana* (smaller-growing, pale yellow flowers).

PLANT PROFILE
HEIGHT 3ft (1m)
SPREAD 5ft (1.5m)
SITE Full sun
SOIL Free-draining
HARDINESS Z8–9 H9–8
FLOWERING Early and midsummer

P | *Photinia* x *fraseri* 'Red Robin'

AN EVERGREEN WITH A DIFFERENCE—at first glance, this beautiful plant's display of rich red, new spring leaves look just like flowers. 'Red Robin' is the best of the photinias for this effect, and with its neat shape it makes an extremely useful shrub for large borders, though it can also be grown as a hedge. Encourage bushiness and even more colorful spring foliage by pruning young plants in late winter. The small, white summer flowers are an extra bonus. Grow in fertile, moist but free-draining soil.

OTHER VARIETIES *P. davidiana* (dark green leaves turn red in autumn, red fruit); *P. davidiana* 'Palette' (slow-growing, creamy white-marked leaves); *P. davidiana* var. *undulata* 'Fructu Luteo' (yellow fruit).

PLANT PROFILE
HEIGHT 15ft (5m)
SPREAD 15ft (5m)
SITE Full sun or partial shade
SOIL Fertile, moist but free-draining
HARDINESS Z8–9 H9–8
FLOWERING Mid- and late spring

Phygelius x *rectus* 'African Queen' Cape fuchsia

P

FOR MOST OF THE SUMMER this exceptionally showy shrub throws up long spikes of small, dangling, orange-red tubular flowers. It needs a sheltered, sunny spot in the garden, and fertile soil with excellent drainage is also a must. Although the foliage is evergreen, in cold winters the topgrowth may die. Don't worry if it does; just cut back stems hard and they should reshoot the following spring. In mild regions where the growth remains healthy over winter, lightly trim for shape in spring.

OTHER VARIETIES *P. aequalis* (smaller, dusky pink flowers with crimson and yellow); *P. aequalis* 'Yellow Trumpet' (creamy yellow flowers, pale green leaves); *P. capensis* (yellow-throated orange flowers).

PLANT PROFILE
HEIGHT 3ft (1m)
SPREAD 4ft (1.2m)
SITE Full sun
SOIL Fertile, moist but free-draining
HARDINESS Z8–9 H9–8
FLOWERING Summer

Phyllostachys aureosulcata 'Aureocaulis' Golden-groove bamboo

ONE OF THE BEST YELLOW-STEMMED bamboos, 'Aureocaulis' offers extra color from occasional green stripes. It makes a superb feature plant, hedge, or screen. For a fun, lively combination, grow it against a beech hedge, where in winter its green leaves will contrast well with the orange-brown beech foliage. It is an invasive type of bamboo, and you must be ruthless in cutting out any shoots that appear where you don't want them—slice them off with a spade. Keep it well away from artificial ponds, since new shoots may spear through the lining material.

OTHER VARIETY *P. bambusoides* 'Allgold' (golden yellow canes, sometimes green-striped, leaves occasionally yellow-striped).

PLANT PROFILE
HEIGHT 10–20ft (3–6m)
SPREAD Indefinite
SITE Full sun or dappled shade
SOIL Fertile, moist but free-draining
HARDINESS Z5–11 H12–3

Physocarpus opulifolius 'Dart's Gold' Ninebark

THE YOUNG LEAVES OF 'DART'S GOLD' are a cheery sight in spring, when they add a dash of bright yellow. In early summer, pink-tinged cup-shaped flowers are followed by tiny red fruits in autumn. Then, in winter, the bark peels off in attractive curls. This deciduous shrub thrives in most well-drained soils—it does particularly well on acidic ones—but results are likely to be disappointing on shallow, alkaline soil. Prune established plants after flowering, cutting one in four of the flowered shoots back to the ground.

PLANT PROFILE

HEIGHT 6ft (2m)

SPREAD 8ft (2.5m)

SITE Full sun or partial shade

SOIL Preferably acidic, free-draining

HARDINESS Z3–7 H7–1

FLOWERING Early summer

P

Pieris 'Forest Flame' Lily-of-the-valley shrub

AN EXCELLENT EVERGREEN SHRUB, 'Forest Flame' stands smartly to attention, adding shape to any winter border. The glossy leaves gradually fade from their late-winter livery of bright red, when they make a strong contrast against the long sprays of white spring flowers, and turn pink and creamy white to end up dark green in summer. Note that 'Forest Flame' must have an acidic soil that is fertile, moist but free-draining. In frost-prone areas it needs shelter from cold winds. To keep a neat shape, trim gently after flowering.

OTHER VARIETIES *P. formosa* var. *forrestii* 'Wakehurst' (brilliant red young leaves); *P. japonica* (clusters of white flowers from late winter).

PLANT PROFILE
HEIGHT 12ft (4m)
SPREAD 6ft (2m)
SITE Full sun or partial shade
SOIL Acidic, fertile, moist but free-draining
HARDINESS Z6–9 H9–6
FLOWERING Mid- and late spring

Pileostegia viburnoides

P

SELF-CLINGING WOODY STEMS enable this evergreen wall shrub to climb without being tied to a trellis or horizontal wires. An old, sturdy tree trunk also makes a perfect climbing frame. The shrub has unbelievably glossy, pointed, bright green leaves—up to 6in (15cm) long—that make a wonderful backdrop for the bright red berries of a cotoneaster or pyracantha. While *Pileostegia viburnoides* grows well in shade, a spot in full sun will encourage it to produce an abundance of broad sprays of tiny, white flowers. It also needs a sheltered site, and can be pruned lightly after flowering for shape and size, if required.

PLANT PROFILE
HEIGHT 20ft (6m)
SITE Sun or shade
SOIL Fertile, free-draining
HARDINESS Z7–11 H12–7
FLOWERING Late summer and autumn

P

Piptanthus nepalensis Evergreen laburnum

RIGHT AT THE START OF SUMMER, this semievergreen shrub is covered from head to toe in pealike flowers. It will suffer if left to the mercy of cold winter winds, so choose a warm, sheltered spot—at the back of a sunny border or against a sun-facing wall would be ideal. After flowering, cut back the flowered stems of wall-grown shrubs to within four buds of the base. When grown as a bush, in late winter prune it by about a third to create an open shape. It will make a sturdy support for climbers, such as clematis—strong blues and clear whites create a striking combination.

OTHER VARIETY *P. tomentosus* (pealike, lemon yellow flowers, followed by woolly seed pods).

PLANT PROFILE
HEIGHT 8ft (2.5m)
SPREAD 6ft (2m)
SITE Full sun or partial shade
SOIL Fertile, free-draining
HARDINESS Z11–15 H12–9
FLOWERING Late spring and early summer

TRAINING

Most pittosporums grow naturally with a single, main stem, which makes them ideal for training as standards.

Pittosporum tenuifolium Kohuhu

P

VERGING ON A SMALL TREE, this shrub has black stems with glossy, wavy edged, fresh green leaves and, in late spring, dark red flowers that smell like honey. Initially narrow in shape, it later broadens out and makes an excellent hedging plant for a warm, sheltered garden in rich, moist but free-draining soil. In colder areas you must provide protection against winter winds. Trim out damaged wood and clip for shape in spring—if you wait until midsummer, the shrub won't have time to recover before winter.

OTHER VARIETIES *P. tenuifolium* 'Silver Queen' (variegated leaves, dark red flowers); *P. tenuifolium* 'Tom Thumb' (shorter, bronze-purple leaves); *P. tenuifolium* 'Warnham Gold' (golden yellow leaves).

PLANT PROFILE
HEIGHT 12–30ft (4–10m)
SPREAD 6–15ft (2–5m)
SITE Full sun or partial shade
SOIL Fertile, moist but free-draining
HARDINESS Z9–11 H12–9
FLOWERING Late spring and early summer

P | *Pleioblastus pygmaeus* var. *distichus* Bamboo

TAKE CARE WITH THIS EVERGREEN BAMBOO. The height suggests it can be grown in a pot or tight space, but it is much too invasive. In fact, the parent, *Pleioblastus pygmaeus*, is so rampant that it quickly colonizes huge areas of ground. However, when used as ground cover in a wild garden, this variety produces a lush and exotic effect, but don't site it near any plants you cherish because they will soon be swamped. Plant it in rich, moist but free-draining soil. In small gardens, try the better-behaved *P. auricomus*.

OTHER VARIETIES *P. humilis* (upright, dark green canes, mid-green leaves sometimes downy beneath); *P. variegatus* (shorter-growing, pale green canes with white nodes, dark green leaves with cream stripes).

PLANT PROFILE
HEIGHT 3ft (1m)
SPREAD 5ft (1.5m)
SITE Full sun or partial shade
SOIL Fertile, moist but free-draining
HARDINESS Z7–10

Poncirus trifoliata Japanese bitter orange

NOTE THE COMMON NAME OF THIS DECIDUOUS SHRUB because, despite the luscious appearance of the fruit, it is bitter and inedible. This is a great shame because as a hardy, fruit-bearing shrub or tree, it would be quite a catch. Still, its strongly scented, white spring flowers are exquisite and more than make up for this shortfall. In autumn, these are followed by the fruit, which, if the site is sunny and sheltered, will ripen from green to orange. Once the fruiting period has finished, you can prune it to any convenient size. It makes a magnificent ornamental hedge, which, thanks to its long, vicious spines, is impenetrable—so plant with caution in gardens used by children. The soil should be rich and free-draining.

PLANT PROFILE
HEIGHT 15ft (5m)
SPREAD 15ft (5m)
SITE Full sun
SOIL Fertile, free-draining
HARDINESS Z5–9 H9–5
FLOWERING Late spring and early summer

P

Potentilla fruticosa 'Red Ace' Shrubby cinquefoil

FOR GAPS, BORDERS, as a mini-hedge or an edging plant, low-growing potentillas offer a great solution. They come in a wide range of colors, including white, pink, yellow, and red—'Red Ace' is especially vibrant with its yellow-backed petals—with single and double flowers. Their season is long, from late spring right through until midautumn, and they are low-maintenance, deciduous plants that are happy in free-draining, average soil. Prune potentillas lightly after flowering to keep them shapely.

OTHER VARIETIES   *P. fruticosa* 'Abbotswood' (white flowers);
P. fruticosa 'Longacre Variety' (lower-growing, bright yellow flowers);
P. fruticosa 'Tangerine' (yellow flowers flushed with pale orange-red).

PLANT PROFILE		
HEIGHT 3ft (1m)		
SPREAD 3ft (1m)		
SITE Full sun		
SOIL Average, free-draining		
HARDINESS Z3–7 H7–1		
FLOWERING Late spring to midautumn		

Prostanthera cuneata **Alpine mint bush**

P

A SUNNY, SHELTERED GARDEN that never gets too cold in winter is essential for this Australian evergreen. The safest place is in well-drained soil at the foot of a south-facing wall, where the plant can bask in the reflected warmth. It has strongly scented leaves and an arresting show of flowers that are delicately freckled inside with mauve and yellow. If you don't have a suitable spot in the garden, grow it in a large container and bring it under cover in the winter. Prune lightly after flowering to retain a neat shape.

OTHER VARIETIES *P. rotundifolia* (larger-growing, lilac purple, bell-shaped flowers); *P. rotundifolia rosea* (light rose pink flowers with mauve centers, gray-green leaves).

PLANT PROFILE
HEIGHT 3ft (1m)
SPREAD 3ft (1m)
SITE Full sun
SOIL Moist but free-draining
HARDINESS Z9–10
FLOWERING Summer

Prunus laurocerasus 'Otto Luyken' Cherry laurel

INDISPUTABLY ONE OF THE BEST CHERRY LAURELS. Although most of them are spring-flowering trees, 'Otto Luyken' is a small, dense, bushy shrub with glossy evergreen leaves that makes a perfect mini-hedge. Spikes of white flowers appear in spring, often with a second flush in autumn. Prune to shape after flowering or at any time over summer, although there's a risk that you may sacrifice the autumn flowers. Very undemanding, it thrives in average, free-draining soil.

OTHER VARIETIES *P.* x *cistena* (taller-growing, white flowers, red-purple leaves); *P. laurocerasus* (taller-growing, fragrant white flowers, cherrylike red fruit); *P. laurocerasus* 'Rotundifolia' (taller-growing, good hedging); *P. spinosa* (taller-growing, white flowers, edible black fruit).

PLANT PROFILE
HEIGHT 3ft (1m)
SPREAD 5ft (1.5m)
SITE Full sun
SOIL Average, free-draining
HARDINESS Z6–9 H9–6
FLOWERING Mid- and late spring

Prunus tenella 'Fire Hill' Dwarf Russian almond

P

SMALL, UPRIGHT AND BUSHY, with many slender stems, 'Fire Hill' is an attractive mix of glossy, dark green leaves and, in spring, richly colored, dark pink flowers. These are followed by gray–yellow fruit. Most deciduous ornamental cherries make extremely large shrubs or trees with sensational spring blossoms and are far too large for the average garden, but 'Fire Hill' is just the right size. In autumn, before leaf fall, the foliage is injected with a dash of orange. It will grow happily in average, free-draining soil.

OTHER VARIETIES *P. glandulosa* 'Sinensis' (double pink flowers); *P. triloba* (taller-growing, solitary or paired pink flowers, red fruit).

PLANT PROFILE
HEIGHT 5ft (1.5m)
SPREAD 5ft (1.5m)
SITE Full sun
SOIL Average, free-draining
HARDINESS Z6–8 H8–6
FLOWERING Mid- and late spring

P | *Ptelea trifoliata* Hop tree

DESPITE ITS COMMON NAME, this is a deciduous shrub rather than a tree. However, it does have a large spread and therefore needs a correspondingly large garden. A woodland setting, perimeter border, or spare piece of ground are all ideal. It has three major assets: first, the flowers are richly scented, as are the leaves when crushed; second, the starlike, greenish-white flowers are followed by winged, flattened, green fruit; and, third, the leaves turn a wonderful yellow before falling in autumn.

OTHER VARIETY *P. trifoliata* 'Aurea' (smaller-growing, bright yellow young leaves, turning green and then reverting to yellow in autumn).

PLANT PROFILE
HEIGHT 25ft (8m)
SPREAD 12ft (4m)
SITE Full sun or dappled shade
SOIL Fertile, free-draining
HARDINESS Z5–9 H9–5
FLOWERING Summer

Pyracantha 'Soleil d'Or' Firethorn

A PROLIFIC SHOW OF GOLDEN BERRIES is reason enough to grow this evergreen firethorn, but enjoy the show while it lasts because the berries are a favorite winter food of garden birds. Vicious thorns make pyracantha a good burglar deterrent, and it is often used as an impenetrable perimeter hedge, or trained flat against a house wall to encircle the windows. Plants need protection from icy winds and prefer a free-draining soil. The best time to prune is midspring, even though this will reduce the amount of flowers and berries.

OTHER VARIETIES *P. coccinea* (taller, creamy white flowers, scarlet berries); *P.* 'Golden Charmer' (bright orange-red berries); *P.* 'Mohave' (taller, red berries); *P.* 'Orange Glow' (dark orange berries).

PLANT PROFILE
HEIGHT 10ft (3m)
SPREAD 8ft (2.5m)
SITE Full sun or partial shade
SOIL Free-draining
HARDINESS Z7–9 H9–7
FLOWERING Early summer

R | *Rhamnus alaternus* 'Argenteovariegata' Italian buckthorn

THIS EXCELLENT, FAST-GROWING EVERGREEN has plenty of yellow-green flowers and tiny red berries, ripening to black, but they don't compete with its major feature—the white-edged foliage. The leaf markings make a lively contrast with red-berrying shrubs, such as cotoneaster or pyracantha, and in an action-packed border they make a strong visual break between different color schemes. Prune buckthorn lightly in early spring and remove any all-green leaves as soon as they appear or the whole plant may turn green.

OTHER VARIETIES *R. cathartica* (dark green leaves turning yellow in autumn, red fruit); *R. frangula* (dark green leaves turning red).

PLANT PROFILE	
HEIGHT 15ft (5m)	
SPREAD 12ft (4m)	
SITE Full sun	
SOIL Free-draining	
HARDINESS Z7–9 H9–7	
FLOWERING Late spring and early summer	

Rhaphiolepis umbellata Indian hawthorn

R

SLOW-GROWING, WITH THICK, LEATHERY, glossy, dark green leaves, *Rhaphiolepis umbellata* makes an extremely versatile border shrub. At the end of spring it is liberally covered in clusters of small, star-shaped, scented flowers that are usually white but sometimes tinged rose pink. Dark blue-black berries follow. Grow it in average soil that's relatively free draining, and position it in a sunny, sheltered site. Clip for shape after flowering.

OTHER VARIETIES *R.* x *delacourii* 'Coates' Crimson' (dark pink flowers); *R.* x *delacourii* 'Enchantress' (dwarf, rose pink flowers); *R. indica* (white flowers with pink-flushed centers).

PLANT PROFILE
HEIGHT 5ft (1.5m)
SPREAD 5ft (1.5m)
SITE Full sun
SOIL Average, moist but free-draining
HARDINESS Z8–11 H12–8
FLOWERING Early summer

R *Rhodochiton atrosanguineus* Purple bell vine

COLORFUL AND CURIOUS, this unusual evergreen climber has dark purple, bell-shaped flowers with long maroon tubes (*see inset*). Given a sunny, sheltered spot it can be grown in the garden, where it is usually treated as an annual. In a warm conservatory border it will safely overwinter as a perennial—just keep watch for red spider mites and whiteflies. Annual spring pruning at the base will force up fresh, vigorous growth. In the garden, you can train it up a pergola or a wall along horizontal wires, or over adjoining shrubs. Once the flowers open in summer, they will keep coming until autumn, as long as the weather holds. Plants are easily raised from seeds sown in spring in small pots on a windowsill.

PLANT PROFILE

HEIGHT 10ft (3m)

SITE Full sun

SOIL Fertile, moist but free-draining

HARDINESS Z12–15 H8–2

FLOWERING Summer to autumn

Rhododendron luteum Pontic azalea

R

IN SPRING, THIS EYE–CATCHING DECIDUOUS AZALEA fills the air with great wafts of honeysuckle-like scent. Given the right conditions—plenty of well-rotted organic matter forked into acidic soil, and bright sun—it is a real bonus in a woodland garden. It looks stunning against a dense carpet of bluebells with its flowers just starting to open on bare, twiggy branches. In autumn, the leaves turn red and orange before falling. Don't disturb the soil around the stem because it is shallow-rooting.

OTHER VARIETIES *R.* 'Berryrose' (smaller-growing, apricot orange flowers); *R.* 'Cecile' (smaller-growing, salmon pink); *R.* 'Gibraltar' (smaller-growing, brilliant orange); *R.* 'Persil' (smaller-growing, white flowers).

PLANT PROFILE

HEIGHT 12ft (4m)

SPREAD 12ft (4m)

SITE Full sun

SOIL Acidic, moist but free-draining

HARDINESS Z7–9 H9–7

FLOWERING Late spring and early summer

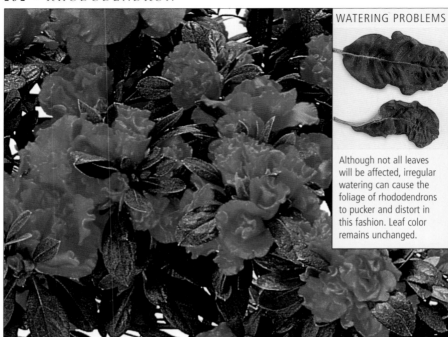

WATERING PROBLEMS

Although not all leaves will be affected, irregular watering can cause the foliage of rhododendrons to pucker and distort in this fashion. Leaf color remains unchanged.

R | *Rhododendron* 'Vuyk's Scarlet' Azalea

BEAUTIFUL, COMPACT, AND EVERGREEN, 'Vuyk's Scarlet' has crimson spring flowers and small, dark green leaves. Like all rhododendrons, it requires acidic soil and plenty of leafy humus in its planting hole. You must also avoid planting it too deep because the roots like to grow just under the surface of the soil. Shade for part of the day is ideal, although this azalea will also grow well in full sun. If the stems of mature plants become tangled, cut them out, and to keep the plant neat, prune in early summer when flowering has finished.

OTHER VARIETIES *R.*'Beethoven' (taller, magenta-pink flowers); *R.* 'Hinode-giri' (bright crimson); *R.* 'Hinomayo' (pink); *R.* 'Kirin' (deep pink to rose pink); *R.* 'Vuyk's Rosyred' (rose, dark pink inside).

PLANT PROFILE

HEIGHT 30in (75cm)

SPREAD 4ft (1.2m)

SITE Partial shade or full sun

SOIL Acidic, moist but free-draining

HARDINESS Z6–9 H9–5

FLOWERING Midspring

Rhodotypos scandens Jetbead

ALTHOUGH MODEST IN SIZE, this is a quality, vertical shrub suitable for medium-sized gardens. It has attractive, crinkled leaves, about 2⅓in (6cm) long, and the papery, four-petaled white flowers appear from late spring (*see inset*), followed by glossy black berries. Under ideal conditions, the flowers and berries will appear together. Grow this shrub in large borders or wild gardens, where its only requirement is decent drainage. Sun is best, but light shade is perfectly acceptable. Give young plants a light trim after flowering, but prune established plants harder to reinvigorate them, removing about one in four of the stems.

R

PLANT PROFILE

HEIGHT 5ft (1.5m)

SPREAD 5ft (1.5m)

SITE Sun

SOIL Moist but free-draining

HARDINESS Z5–8 H8–5

FLOWERING Late spring and early summer

R | *Rhus typhina* 'Dissecta' Staghorn sumac

DON'T CONFUSE THIS PLANT with its parent *Rhus typhina*, which is a 15ft- (5m-) high tree. 'Dissecta' is shrubbier but has the same attractive, furry, reddish new shoots, followed by yellow–green flowers in summer. Its best season is autumn, when it has clusters of plumelike, hairy crimson fruit, while the long dangling leaves, each one beautifully divided, turn arresting shades of orange-red before falling (*see inset*). It makes a colorful feature or informal perimeter shrub, and needs moist but free-draining soil.

OTHER VARIETIES *R. aromatica* (shorter, leaves turn orange to red–purple); *R. copallina* (shorter, leaves turn bright red); *R. glabra* (leaves turn rich red); *R. x pulvinata* 'Red Autumn Lace' (leaves turn red-purple).

PLANT PROFILE
HEIGHT 6ft (2m)
SPREAD 10ft (3m)
SITE Full sun
SOIL Average, moist but free-draining
HARDINESS Z3–8 H8–1
FLOWERING Summer

Ribes sanguineum 'King Edward VII' Flowering currant

R

DESPITE ITS TEMPTING COMMON NAME, this currant is ornamental and its tiny blue-black berries are inedible. The main attraction of this compact, deciduous shrub is the hanging clusters of dark red, tubular flowers that appear in spring. It's not very fussy and will thrive on average soil, as long as it's free-draining. To retain a good shape, prune immediately after flowering, cutting any old, woody stems back to the ground.

OTHER VARIETIES *R. sanguineum* (pink flowers, blue-black fruit); *R. sanguineum* 'Brocklebankii' (slow-growing, pale pink flowers, bright yellow leaves); *R. sanguineum* 'Tydeman's White' (taller-growing, white flowers); *R. speciosum* (dark red flowers, red fruit).

PLANT PROFILE

HEIGHT 6ft (2m)

SPREAD 6ft (2m)

SITE Full sun

SOIL Average, free-draining

HARDINESS Z6–8 H8–6

FLOWERING Spring

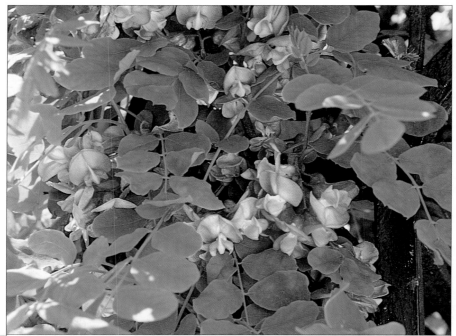

R | *Robinia hispida* Rose acacia

A COLORFUL DECIDUOUS SHRUB for poor, dry soils. Dark green leaves provide a perfect backdrop for the dangling clusters of rose pink flowers that cover the arching stems in early summer. These are followed by prickly brown seed pods from which the bristly locust gets its name. Tie the fragile branches securely to horizontal wires fixed to a warm wall or fence, since they can easily snap in strong winds. Alternatively, it will grow well as a border shrub in a very sheltered garden.

OTHER VARIETY *R. kelseyi* (smaller-growing, bright rose pink flowers).

PLANT PROFILE
HEIGHT 8ft (2.5m)
SPREAD 10ft (3m)
SITE Full sun
SOIL Poor, dry, free-draining
HARDINESS Z6–11 H12–6
FLOWERING Late spring and early summer

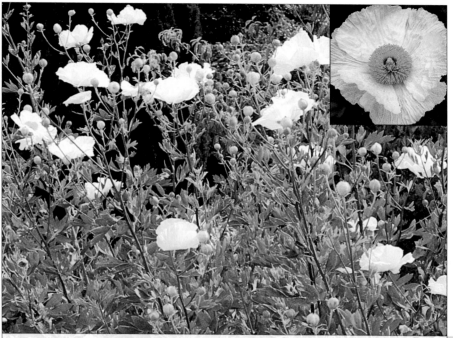

Romneya coulteri Matilija poppy

R

THIS SURPRISE MEMBER OF THE POPPY FAMILY bears white, gently scented flowers with yellow centers that look like poached eggs (*see inset*) and appear over a long period. The deeply cut, gray-green leaves are also very attractive. The Matilija poppy has a reputation for being slow to take off, but it soon makes a substantial plant with new stems growing straight out of the ground. Choose a sunny, sheltered spot for it on rich, free-draining soil, and cover the crown of the plant with a thick mulch of compost over winter. If the stems get frosted, just cut them down to the ground in early spring and they'll soon grow back.

OTHER VARIETY *R. coulteri* 'White Cloud' (glaucous leaves).

PLANT PROFILE
HEIGHT 3–8ft (1–2.5m)
SPREAD Indefinite
SITE Full sun
SOIL Fertile, free-draining
HARDINESS Z8–10 H9–2
FLOWERING Summer

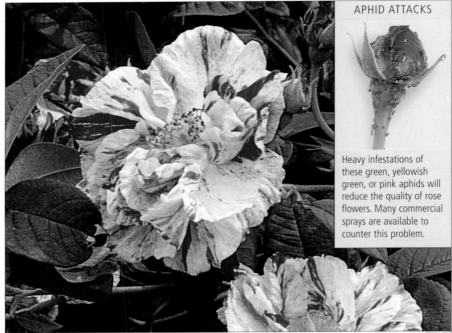

APHID ATTACKS

APHID ATTACKS

Heavy infestations of these green, yellowish green, or pink aphids will reduce the quality of rose flowers. Many commercial sprays are available to counter this problem.

R

Rosa gallica var. *officinalis* 'Versicolor' Rosa Mundi rose

NAMED AFTER HENRY II'S MISTRESS, "the Fair Rosamond," this small and showy, red-and-pink striped rose predates the 17th century. It belongs to a group of sweet-smelling, old garden roses called the Gallicas that flower only once in summer, although that display is nothing short of spectacular. Grow it as a single specimen or as a mini-hedge to inject color into formal and informal planting plans. A typical rose, it is a hungry feeder and craves rich, moist but free-draining soil. Prune only to reduce sideshoots by two-thirds, and overly long shoots by up to one-third.

OTHER VARIETIES *R.* 'Belle de Crécy' (taller, double, pink to purple flowers); *R.* 'Tuscany Superb' (double, crimson to maroon flowers).

PLANT PROFILE	
HEIGHT 32in (80cm)	
SPREAD 3ft (1m)	
SITE Full sun	
SOIL Fertile, moist but free-draining	
HARDINESS Z3–9 H9–1	
FLOWERING Summer	

Rosa 'Golden Showers' Modern climbing rose

R

LIKE ALL CLIMBING ROSES, the scented, double-flowering 'Golden Showers' performs best when trained on horizontal wires fixed to a wall, or grown around a pillar or post. This training forces new flowering growth along the main stems. If it is trained straight up, lower growth will be bare and flowers will be borne near the top of the plant. Climbers usually have stiff stems, and plants over three years old should by pruned by cutting back sideshoots by two-thirds after flowering. All roses prefer rich, moist but free-draining soil.

OTHER VARIETIES *R.* 'Gloire de Dijon' (taller, double, creamy buff flowers); *R.* 'Guinée' (shorter, double, blackish red flowers); *R.* 'Mermaid' (taller, single, primrose yellow flowers).

PLANT PROFILE
HEIGHT 10ft (3m)
SITE Full sun or partial shade
SOIL Fertile, moist but free-draining
HARDINESS Z5–9 H9–5
FLOWERING Summer to autumn

R

Rosa moyesii 'Geranium' Wild rose

WHERE SPACE ALLOWS, *Rosa moyesii* 'Geranium' is one of the best of the flowering wild roses, although it is a little too large for a small garden. Its assets include fresh green leaves, outstanding, rich red flowers, and large, orange-red hips (*see inset*). A growth habit that is smartly erect means it will keep to its allotted space in the border without sprawling over other plants. Virtually thornless, it also makes a beautiful ornamental hedge. Grow it in rich, moist but free-draining soil; restrict pruning to removing dead wood in spring.

OTHER VARIETIES *R.* 'Complicata' (single, pink flowers); *R. macrophylla* (taller-growing, single, fragrant, red flowers); *R. moyesii* (taller-growing, single, scarlet flowers).

PLANT PROFILE

HEIGHT 8ft (2.5m)

SPREAD 5ft (1.5m)

SITE Full sun

SOIL Fertile, moist but free-draining

HARDINESS Z4–9 H9–1

FLOWERING Summer

Rosa 'Nevada' Shrub rose

R

FEW ROSES CAN RIVAL 'NEVADA' in early summer, when its stems are covered with creamy white flowers, each about 4in (10cm) across. Among the dense green leaves there are glimpses of vibrant reddish brown arching stems. After deadheading the first flush of flowers, if the weather stays warm and sunny, a second sprinkling of buds will open in autumn. Once flowering is finally finished, prune the main stems by up to a third, and the sideshoots by a half to two-thirds. A rich, moist but free-draining soil suits it best.

OTHER VARIETIES *R.* 'Cerise Bouquet' (taller, semidouble, cherry red flowers); *R.* 'Frühlingsgold' (semidouble, fragrant, pale yellow flowers); *R.* 'Scharlachglut' (taller, single, crimson-scarlet flowers).

PLANT PROFILE
HEIGHT 7ft (2.2m)
SPREAD 7ft (2.2m)
SITE Full sun
SOIL Fertile, moist but free-draining
HARDINESS Z4–9 H9–1
FLOWERING Early summer and autumn

BLIND SHOOTS

On any rose, shorten shoots without a terminal flower bud by about half, cutting to an outward-facing bud. These blind shoots divert the plant's energy if left unpruned.

R *Rosa* 'Rambling Rector' Multiflora rambler rose

RAMBLERS CAN BE GROWN IN TWO WAYS: you can let them clamber into a tree, eventually becoming a tangle of stems; or you can keep them neater and more floriferous by growing them around a pillar or pergola. Either way, 'Rambling Rector' produces arching stems with small, sweetly scented flowers followed by red hips. Prune established plants after flowering, cutting one in three flowered stems back to the ground. Cut sideshoots back to two or four buds.

OTHER VARIETIES *R.* 'Bobbie James' (taller-growing, semidouble, fragrant, cream flowers); *R.* 'Crimson Shower' (smaller-growing, double, crimson flowers); *R.* 'Goldfinch' (smaller-growing, double, fragrant, deep yellow flowers); *R.* 'Veilchenblau' (double, fruit-scented, violet flowers).

PLANT PROFILE
HEIGHT 20ft (6m)
SITE Full sun
SOIL Fertile, moist but free-draining
HARDINESS Z5–9 H9–5
FLOWERING Summer

Rosa 'William Lobb' Moss rose

R

THIS ATTRACTIVE ROSE DOES A QUICK COLOR CHANGE: the flowers open a deep purple and then, within 24 hours, turn lavender-gray, giving a striking two-tone effect. 'William Lobb' is a Moss rose, so called because of the furry growth that covers its graceful arching stems. Grow it in a sheltered border so that its sweet perfume will linger in the still air —close to the house against a sunny patio wall would be perfect. Plant it in fertile, moist but well-drained soil, and prune lightly immediately after flowering.

OTHER VARIETY *R.* 'Nuits de Young' (Moss rose, double, fragrant, maroon-purple flowers with yellow stamens).

PLANT PROFILE
HEIGHT 6ft (2m)
SPREAD 6ft (2m)
SITE Full sun
SOIL Fertile, moist but free-draining
HARDINESS Z4–9 H9–1
FLOWERING Summer

R *Rosmarinus officinalis* 'Severn Sea' Rosemary

ROSEMARY CULTIVARS SHOW GREAT VARIETY IN HABIT: there are upright ones that are ideal for hedging (such as 'Miss Jessopp's Upright'), while others are spreading and prostrate (such as 'Prostratus') and make surprisingly good groundcover. 'Severn Sea' veers toward a bushy type of growth, with arching branches, and it responds well to being gently pruned in spring to give it an open shape. All like full sun, which intensifies the flavor of the leaves, and average, free-draining soil. If you don't regularly snip your rosemary for potpourri and cooking, then give it a gentle trim after flowering.

OTHER VARIETIES *R. officinalis* 'Roseus' (pink flowers); *R. officinalis* 'Tuscan Blue' (dark blue flowers).

PLANT PROFILE
HEIGHT 3ft (1m)
SPREAD 3ft (1m)
SITE Full sun
SOIL Average, free-draining
HARDINESS Z8–11 H12–8
FLOWERING Midspring to early summer

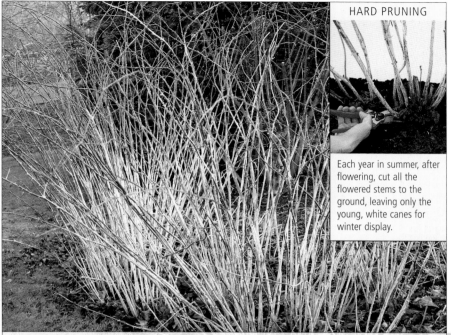

HARD PRUNING

Each year in summer, after flowering, cut all the flowered stems to the ground, leaving only the young, white canes for winter display.

Rubus cockburnianus Bramble

R

MENTION THE WORD "BRAMBLE" and gardeners visibly shudder, but this ornamental one is relatively tame. Still, it's most suitable for a wild or woodland garden where it will make a thicket of deciduous stems. In winter, the young, bare shoots are covered in a white, waxy powder, while in summer it produces tiny purple flowers followed by small, inedible berries. To encourage new white stems in winter, cut back all stems to within two or three buds of the base in early spring; alternatively, to retain some flowering stems, in summer cut down only those stems that have just bloomed.

PLANT PROFILE	
HEIGHT	8ft (2.5m)
SPREAD	8ft (2.5m)
SITE	Full sun
SOIL	Average, free-draining
HARDINESS	Z6–8 H8–6
FLOWERING	Summer

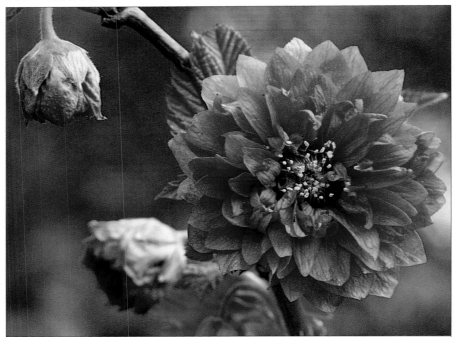

R | *Rubus spectabilis* 'Olympic Double' Salmonberry

DECIDUOUS AND THICKET-FORMING, the beautiful, ornamental bramble 'Olympic Double' is grown for its 2in- (5cm-) wide purple-pink, double flowers. Opening in spring when the leaves appear, they are highly visible thanks to their fine coloring and the fact that the stems are still relatively bare. It is best grown in a wild or woodland garden and prefers average, free-draining soil. Prune after flowering, cutting back flowered shoots to vigorous buds. When established, also cut back about one in four of the old shoots to the base, forcing up new, vigorous growth.

OTHER VARIETIES *R.* 'Benenden' (roselike, white flowers in late spring and early summer); *R. thibetanus* (red-purple flowers in summer).

PLANT PROFILE	
HEIGHT 6ft (2m)	
SPREAD 6ft (2m)	
SITE Full sun	
SOIL Average, free-draining	
HARDINESS Z5–8 H8–5	
FLOWERING Midspring	

Ruta graveolens 'Jackman's Blue' Common rue

R

THE SMALL, COMPACT LEAVES of this evergreen have a gorgeous blue tinge. Grow it at the foot of bright red and pastel roses or along the edge of a straight path where it will spill over to soften the hard lines, but do bear in mind that contact with the leaves can cause skin irritation. Many gardeners consider the pale yellow flowers to be a distraction and shear the plant in spring to reduce their numbers. Because it needs sharp drainage and thrives in hot sites, the plant is suitable for growing in Mediterranean-style or gravel gardens. It is frequently grown in herb gardens, since herbalists use its leaves in various preparations, but it is poisonous if eaten.

OTHER VARIETY *R. graveolens* (taller-growing).

PLANT PROFILE
HEIGHT 24in (60cm)
SPREAD 30in (75cm)
SITE Full sun or partial shade
SOIL Free-draining
HARDINESS Z5–9 H9–5
FLOWERING Summer

Salix alba subsp. *vitellina* 'Britzensis' White willow

UNLIKE MANY WILLOWS that are grown for their impressive size, some reaching 15m (50ft), 'Britzensis' should be coppiced every one to three years to restrict its height and force up the beautiful, bright red new shoots that are its chief asset. The color is particularly striking when seen against a clear blue winter sky, and it should be positioned with this in mind. Cut the stems back hard in early spring, after the decorative yellow-green catkins have appeared, to produce a tracery of long, thin, almost vertical stems. For best results, grow in rich, moist but well-drained soil.

PLANT PROFILE
HEIGHT 12ft (4m)
SPREAD 12ft (4m)
SITE Full sun
SOIL Fertile, moist but free-draining
HARDINESS Z4–9 H9–1
FLOWERING Early spring

Salix hastata 'Wehrhahnii' Willow

S

BARE, DARK PURPLE STEMS hung with a multitude of silver-gray catkins make this deciduous shrub an exciting addition to the early-spring garden. When the leaves appear, they are bright green. Unlike many tall-growing willows, this is a small shrub that is suitable for most gardens. To create a balance between old wood (bearing catkins) and new wood (giving the best-colored stems), each year cut one in three stems to within two to three buds of the base. Grow in any moist soil, except shallow, chalky ground.

OTHER VARIETIES *S. caprea* 'Kilmarnock' (yellow-brown shoots, gray catkins); *S. fargesii* (glossy green shoots, slender green catkins); *S. lanata* (white-woolly shoots, yellow catkins).

PLANT PROFILE	
HEIGHT	3ft (1m)
SPREAD	3ft (1m)
SITE	Sun
SOIL	Moist but free-draining
HARDINESS	Z5–8 H8–5
FLOWERING	Early spring

S

Salvia officinalis 'Purpurascens' Purple sage

AN ESSENTIAL PLANT FOR A SUNNY HERB GARDEN, sage is grown for its aromatic, evergreen leaves. For culinary purposes, one bushy plant is sufficient for even the most avid cook. The parent, *Salvia officinalis*, is a rather dull green, but other varieties have good leaf color, and 'Purpurascens' is one of the best because its new foliage is an intense reddish purple. Protect young plants in their first few winters—initially, pot them in autumn and bring indoors. Free-draining soil and a sheltered site are essential.

OTHER VARIETIES *S. officinalis* 'Aurea' (purple-blue flowers, yellow leaves); *S. officinalis* 'Icterina' (yellow and green variegated leaves); *S. officinalis* 'Kew Gold' (golden yellow leaves flecked with green).

PLANT PROFILE
HEIGHT 32in (80cm)
SPREAD 3ft (1m)
SITE Full sun to light shade
SOIL Free-draining
HARDINESS Z4–10 H10–1
FLOWERING Early and midsummer

Sambucus nigra 'Guincho Purple' European elder

S

THE WILD GARDEN is the natural home for this deciduous elder. It is grown for the bracing color contrast of tiny, pink-tinged white flowers against a backdrop of dark leaves, which are green in spring, turning blackish purple and then red in autumn. The flowers are followed by tiny black berries that can be cooked and eaten. For the best show of colored leaves, cut all stems to the ground in winter, or remove the old ones and prune the young stems back by half. Elders grow well in most soils.

OTHER VARIETIES   *S. nigra* 'Aurea' (yellow leaves on pink-flushed stalks); *S. nigra* f. *laciniata* (irregularly, finely cut leaflets); *S. racemosa* 'Sutherland Gold' (bronze young leaves turning golden yellow).

PLANT PROFILE
HEIGHT 20ft (6m)
SPREAD 20ft (6m)
SITE Full sun or partial shade
SOIL Average, moist but free-draining
HARDINESS Z6–8 H8–6
FLOWERING Early summer

S

Santolina chamaecyparissus Lavender cotton

THE FRONT OF THE BORDER is where this compact, mound-forming plant will make the greatest impact. Try planting it in rows as a low hedge to edge a path, or in a block to make a very effective groundcover. In summer, buttonlike yellow flowers appear in great numbers (*see inset*), although some people prefer to shear them off so that they don't detract from the silvery gray leaves and stems. The cool shades of cotton lavender make it a good gap-filler for predominantly white borders.

OTHER VARIETIES *S. chamaecyparissus* 'Lemon Queen' (lemon yellow flowers); *S. chamaecyparissus* 'Small-Ness' (dwarf, perfect for rockeries); *S. rosmarinifolia* subsp. *rosmarinifolia* 'Primrose Gem' (pale yellow flowers).

PLANT PROFILE
HEIGHT 20in (50cm)
SPREAD 3ft (1m)
SITE Full sun
SOIL Poor to average, free-draining
HARDINESS Z6–9 H9–5
FLOWERING Mid- and late summer

Sarcococca confusa Christmas boxwood

S

A STRONG, SWEET SCENT IN MIDWINTER is the best reason to include this evergreen in the garden. The scented white flowers are followed by tiny black berries. Christmas boxwood—so named because its leaves resemble those of *Buxus* (boxwood)—is easily grown in average, free-draining soil, and will survive dry shade and a degree of neglect. Young plants grow well in containers—flank the front door with a matching pair in terracotta pots. Maintenance is minimal—just a spring pruning to maintain an attractive shape.

OTHER VARIETIES *S. hookeriana* (spreading, fragrant, white flowers, blue-black fruit); *S. hookeriana* var. *humilis* (smaller, fragrant, pink-white flowers, blue-black fruit); *S. ruscifolia* (smaller, dark red fruit).

PLANT PROFILE	
HEIGHT 6ft (2m)	
SPREAD 3ft (1m)	
SITE Deep or partial shade	
SOIL Average, moist but free-draining	
HARDINESS Z6–9 H9–6	
FLOWERING Winter	

S

Sasa veitchii Kuma-zasa bamboo

A MODERATELY INVASIVE BAMBOO, *Sasa veitchii*'s short, dense, leafy
growth makes wonderful groundcover for wild and wooded areas of
the garden. The dark green, glossy leaves develop distinctive white
margins in winter, and are held horizontally from the purple-green
canes. *Sasa veitchii* f. *minor* is worth tracking down because its slightly
smaller leaves carry even stronger white margins, and it is also
markedly shorter. Both grow well in most ordinary soils, and to
restrict their spread, you can plant them in an open-bottomed pit
lined with paving stones.

OTHER VARIETY *S. palmata* f. *nebulosa* (larger-growing, purple-
streaked canes, glossy bright green leaves with yellow midribs).

PLANT PROFILE
HEIGHT 3–4ft (1–1.2m)
SPREAD Indefinite
SITE Full sun to deep shade
SOIL Fertile, moist but free-draining
HARDINESS Z6–15 H12–1

Schizophragma hydrangeoides Japanese hydrangea vine

S

SELF-CLINGING CLIMBERS like this one don't require horizontal wires or trellises to help them on their way; instead, they need a sturdy, solid surface, such as a tree or wall, for their suckers to latch on to. *Schizophragma hydrangeoides* is a vigorous, deciduous climber with stems thickly cloaked in 6in- (15cm-) long, dark green leaves. In a sunny position it will produce masses of tiny white flowers in large sprays up to 10in (25cm) wide. Even if it is trained against a shady wall, it will still throw out the odd spray. Prune in early spring by cutting back sideshoots to just three buds.

OTHER VARIETIES *S. hydrangeoides* 'Roseum' (white flowers with pink bracts); *S. integrifolium* (white flowers with creamy bracts).

PLANT PROFILE
HEIGHT 40ft (12m)
SITE Full sun or partial shade
SOIL Moist but free-draining
HARDINESS Z6–9 H9–6
FLOWERING Midsummer

S | *Semiarundinaria fastuosa* Narihira bamboo

TALL, MILITARY-STRAIGHT STEMS are typical of this type of bamboo. In cool climates, while it will almost always reach its full height, there's little risk of it spreading sideways and becoming invasive. Plant it as a dense but controllable perimeter screen (chop unwanted sections out with a spade), although if left unchecked—say, in a wild garden—in time it will make impressive clumps or groves. When young, the thick, shiny canes are green with purple-brown stripes, but as they age, especially if grown in full sun, the green is gradually lost. For best results, grow in rich, moist but free-draining soil.

OTHER VARIETIES *S. kagamiana* (shorter, good for clipping); *S. fastuosa* var. *viridis* (taller-growing, canes stay a lighter color).

PLANT PROFILE
HEIGHT 23ft (7m)
SPREAD 6ft (2m)
SITE Full sun or light shade
SOIL Fertile, moist but free-draining
HARDINESS Z6–9 H9–6

Senecio viravira Dusty miller

S

A FIRST-RATE, SILVERY, EVERGREEN SHRUB with elegant, open growth and finely divided leaves. Some gardeners feel that the pale yellow, late-summer flowers detract from the plant's overall appearance and cut them off before they open. It is a popular foliage choice for white planting plans. Because the plant is not reliably hardy, it needs a mild, sheltered position—for example, in a Mediterranean-style courtyard or against a sunny wall. Average soil is fine, but it must be free-draining.

OTHER VARIETIES *S. cineraria* 'Silver Dust' (lacy, near-white leaves); *S. cineraria* 'White Diamond' (oaklike, gray-white leaves).

PLANT PROFILE
HEIGHT 24in (60cm)
SPREAD 3ft (1m)
SITE Full sun
SOIL Average, free-draining
HARDINESS Z8–10 H10–1
FLOWERING Summer to autumn

S

Shibataea kumasasa Okame-zasa bamboo

THERE ARE MANY BAMBOOS available for small spaces, and this noninvasive, clump-forming type can be clipped into a small, neat, leafy mound, or grown in a row to edge the front of a border or path. Its short-jointed, greenish brown canes and rich green leaves will bring a welcome lushness to a gravel garden—during the summer, however, it will need regular watering. The foliage may become damaged during a severe winter, but it will quickly recover the following spring. Unless you can replicate the conditions of its native habit in China and Japan, flowering is extremely rare: in Europe there was only a single recorded case in the 20th century.

PLANT PROFILE

HEIGHT 24–60in (60–150cm)

SPREAD 24in (60cm)

SITE Partial shade or full sun

SOIL Average, moist but free-draining

HARDINESS Z6–15 H12–1

Skimmia japonica 'Rubella'

S

INTERESTING THINGS start to happen to this plant in midwinter, when the red-brown flower buds fatten up. By spring, you'll have a good show of tiny, white, scented flowers. 'Rubella' is a male plant and will not bear berries—plant a female skimmia close by for those—but the red-edged, dark green leaves provide year–round color. Because it can withstand the effects of both sea spray and city pollution, it is a hedging plant. Help plants along by giving them moist, rich, acidic soil. Clip for shape after flowering, if necessary.

OTHER VARIETIES *S. japonica* (male and female, fragrant white flowers often pink-tinged, aromatic leaves); *S. japonica* 'Fragrans' (smaller-growing, free-flowering male); *S. japonica* 'Veitchii' (female form).

PLANT PROFILE	
HEIGHT 20ft (6m)	
SPREAD 20ft (6m)	
SITE Partial or full shade	
SOIL Acidic, moist, fertile	
HARDINESS Z7–9 H9–7	
FLOWERING Spring	

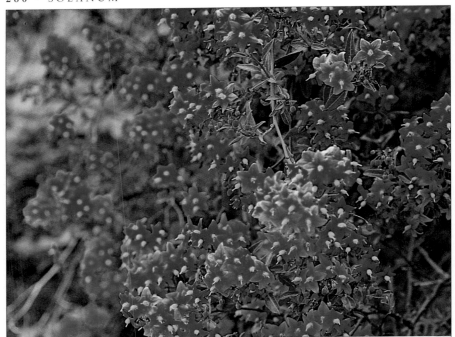

S

Solanum crispum 'Glasnevin' Chilean potato tree

GIVEN SOMEWHERE TO SCRAMBLE, this evergreen or semievergreen climber quickly forms a mass of flowering stems. Yellow-centered, purple-blue flowers appear through summer and well into late autumn; these are followed by yellow-white berries. The plant looks stunning planted with a white or yellow clematis. It prefers the warmth of a sunny wall and needs well-drained soil. To stop the stems from flopping forward or breaking in the wind, tie them to horizontal wires. If necessary, thin out stems in spring and, in cases of severe congestion, cut back hard into the old wood.

OTHER VARIETIES *S. crispum* (lilac- to purple-blue flowers); *S. laciniatum* (smaller-growing, dark blue flowers, bright orange fruit).

PLANT PROFILE
HEIGHT 20ft (6m)
SITE Full sun
SOIL Free-draining
HARDINESS Z9–15 H12–1
FLOWERING Summer to autumn

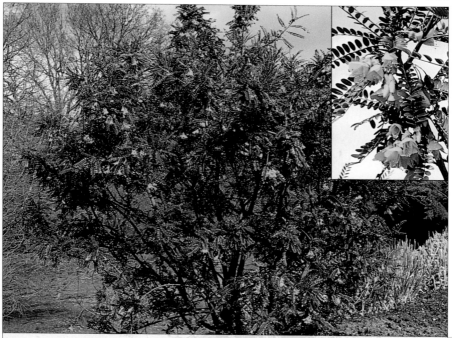

Sophora microphylla 'Sun King' Kowhai

ORIGINALLY FROM THE DRY VALLEYS of tropical regions, this evergreen shrub is equally happy in a woodland garden or sunny border; it also works well as a focal plant. Grown principally for its elegant leaves and dangling clusters of yellow, pealike flowers, it makes a medium-sized, open bush. The flowers are long-lasting and start to make their mark from late winter. 'Sun King' benefits from a warm, protected position in the garden—for example, at the base of a south-facing wall. The hotter the summer, the better the display of flowers is likely to be. Average, well-drained soil and a sunny position will ensure that this shrub thrives.

PLANT PROFILE	
HEIGHT 10ft (3m)	
SPREAD 10ft (3m)	
SITE Full sun	
SOIL Average, free-draining	
HARDINESS Z8–11 H1–12	
FLOWERING Late winter and early spring	

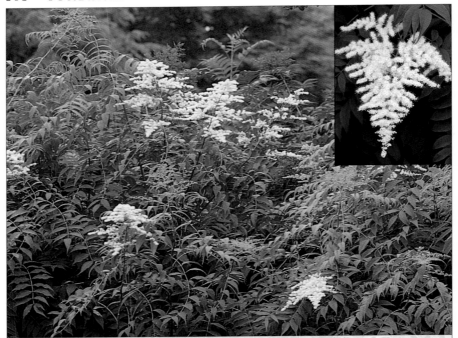

S | *Sorbaria sorbifolia* Ural false spirea

A LARGE BORDER OR A WILD, WOODLAND GARDEN is the perfect home for this versatile, multistemmed plant. It makes an upright deciduous shrub with a spread that is almost twice that of its height. Exuberant white flower plumes (*see inset*) appear in summer above the ornamental foliage. When flowering is over, give the shrub a light all-over pruning to help retain a good shape; alternatively, in spring, cut back hard to near the base to encourage fresh new growth. Remove unwanted suckers to restrict the plant's spread. Tolerant of light shade, it grows best in rich, moist but free-draining soil.

OTHER VARIETIES *S. tomentosa* (taller-growing, white flowers, lance-shaped leaves); *S. tomentosa* var. *angustifolia* (taller-growing, red shoots).

PLANT PROFILE

HEIGHT 6ft (2m)

SPREAD 10ft (3m)

SITE Full sun to partial shade

SOIL Fertile, moist but free-draining

HARDINESS Z2–9 H9–1

FLOWERING Mid- and late summer

Sorbus reducta Dwarf mountain ash

MOST SORBUSES ARE TREES, renowned for their colorful berries and autumn foliage, but *Sorbus reducta* is a multistemmed, suckering shrub. Its size makes it ideal for a large shrub border, wild garden, or woodland setting. In late spring, small white flowers appear, followed by round, crimson berries that age to pinky white. Before falling in autumn, the glossy, dark green leaves turn glorious shades of red and purple. Rich, free-draining, acidic to neutral soil suits it best, but it will tolerate a range of conditions.

OTHER VARIETIES *S. cashmiriana* (taller-growing, white berries); *S. commixta* (taller-growing, red berries, yellow to red autumn leaf color); *S. megalocarpa* (taller-growing, russet-brown berries).

PLANT PROFILE
HEIGHT 3–5ft (1–1.5m)
SPREAD 6ft (2m)
SITE Full sun or dappled shade
SOIL Acidic to neutral, fertile, free-draining
HARDINESS Z5–8 H8–4
FLOWERING Late spring

S — *Spartium junceum* Spanish broom

STIFF, VERTICAL BROOM IS A PLANT FOR ALL SEASONS. In winter it is covered with tiny evergreen leaves, and then, from early summer to autumn, these are joined by masses of fragrant, pealike yellow flowers followed by long, dark brown seed pods. It is suitable for a shrub border and will also grow happily against a warm, sunny wall or fence. As long as it has well-drained soil, broom is extremely tough—it even thrives in exposed coastal gardens, and will also grow well on alkaline soils. With age, if the shrub becomes too spindly, cut it back hard (but not into the oldest wood) to promote new, bushy growth.

PLANT PROFILE

HEIGHT 10ft (3m)

SPREAD 10ft (3m)

SITE Full sun

SOIL Fertile, free-draining

HARDINESS Z8–11 H12–8

FLOWERING Early summer to early autumn

Spiraea 'Arguta' Bridal wreath

IN SPRING, 'ARGUTA' ERUPTS into a mass of white flowers, making it an invaluable feature plant for a sunny border. It can also be included in a mixed hedge beside summer-flowering *Spiraea japonica*. Given an open, sunny position it will thrive in most gardens. After flowering, prune away old or spindly wood. When trimming a mixed spiraea hedge, bear in mind that spring-flowering types bloom on the previous year's growth and summer-flowering ones on the current year's growth.

OTHER VARIETIES *S. japonica* 'Anthony Waterer' (smaller-growing, dark pink flowers, leaves edged with creamy-white are bronze-red when young); *S. japonica* 'Little Princess' (ground cover, rose-pink flowers).

PLANT PROFILE
HEIGHT 8ft (2.5m)
SPREAD 8ft (2.5m)
SITE Full sun
SOIL Fertile, moist but free-draining
HARDINESS Z5–8 H8–5
FLOWERING Spring

S

Spiraea japonica 'Anthony Waterer'

PRODUCING FLAT SPRAYS of dark pink flowers, up to 8in (20cm) across, this very popular deciduous shrub also features dark green leaves, often with a creamy white margin. The young spring leaves are reddish bronze. It is best grown as an informal hedge or in a shrub border, and will thrive in most garden situations as long as extremes of wet and dry soil are avoided. After planting, give the stems a hard pruning, reducing them to about 6in (15cm) above the ground. In future years, prune in the same way each spring, although for a permanent hedge you may prefer to prune less severely.

OTHER VARIETIES *S. japonica* 'Nana' (smaller, dark pink flowers); *S. japonica* 'Shirobana' (smaller, white and dark pink flowers on same plant).

PLANT PROFILE
HEIGHT 5ft (1.5m)
SPREAD 5ft (1.5m)
SITE Full sun
SOIL Fertile, moist but free-draining
HARDINESS Z3–9 H9–1
FLOWERING Mid- and late summer

Spiraea nipponica 'Snowmound'

S

PLENTY OF SPREADING SPACE IS REQUIRED for this fast-growing, deciduous shrub. Plan ahead when planting, because just a few years down the line it will engulf anything in its path. In midsummer it puts on a wonderful show of flat, white flower sprays borne on arching branches. In spring, cut back spent flowering stems to strong buds; on established plants, cut back about a quarter of the old growth to the ground.

OTHER VARIETIES *S. japonica* (pink or white flowers); *S. nipponica* 'Halward's Silver' (smaller-growing); *S. thunbergii* (stalkless white flowers); *S. x vanhouttei* (smaller, compact, white flowers, diamond-shaped leaves).

PLANT PROFILE	
HEIGHT 4–8ft (1.2–2.5m)	
SPREAD 4–8ft (1.2–2.5m)	
SITE Full sun	
SOIL Fertile, moist but free-draining	
HARDINESS Z4–9 H9–1	
FLOWERING Midsummer	

S

Stachyurus praecox Spiketail

AN UNUSUAL DECIDUOUS SHRUB for a woodland setting or growing against a wall, *Stachyurus praecox* is popular for its colorful stems and early flowers that will brighten up the late winter garden. Yellow buds form on its dark red-purple arching stems in autumn, then toward the end of winter, before the long, mid-green leaves appear, nodding rows of tiny, pale yellow-green flowers open. It's a breathtaking combination. Grow in rich, moist but well-drained, acidic soil and provide protection from cold, drying winds. No regular pruning is required; just cut back for shape when necessary.

OTHER VARIETIES *S. chinensis* (bell-shaped, pale yellow flowers); *S.* 'Magpie' (smaller-growing, white leaf margins).

PLANT PROFILE

HEIGHT 3–12ft (1–4m)

SPREAD 10ft (3m)

SITE Partial shade

SOIL Preferably acidic, fertile, moist but free-draining

HARDINESS Z7–9 H9–7

FLOWERING Late winter and early spring

Staphylea pinnata Bladdernut

S

IT'S A GREAT SHAME that this upright, deciduous shrub isn't more generally popular. It is at its best in late spring and early summer, when drooping clusters of lightly scented, creamy white flowers appear among the dark green leaves on its sturdy stems. Strange-looking, greenish white, capsulelike berries follow in autumn. Bladdernut is an easy-care shrub that will grow in most gardens—average soil is fine as long as it never dries out. Clip it after flowering to keep it neat.

OTHER VARIETIES *S. colchica* (smaller-growing, fragrant white flowers, greenish white berries); *S. holocarpa* 'Rosea' (larger-growing, pink flowers, bronze young leaves).

PLANT PROFILE	
HEIGHT 15ft (5m)	
SPREAD 15ft (5m)	
SITE Full sun or partial shade	
SOIL Average, moist	
HARDINESS Z6–9 H9–6	
FLOWERING Late spring and early summer	

S

Stauntonia hexaphylla Japanese staunton vine

THIS EVERGREEN WOODY CLIMBER from the Far East is a real conversation piece. Handsome, dark green leathery leaves, up to 6in (15cm) long, are carried on fast-growing, twining stems. In spring it produces delicately scented, violet-tinged, white bell-shaped flowers followed, after a long hot summer, by sausagelike, edible purple fruit, 2in (5cm) long or more—although you need male and female plants for pollination. If grown in a cool greenhouse border or conservatory
it will climb to 30ft (10m); outdoors, in cooler garden conditions, growth will be more modest. Choose a sunny, sheltered site—against a south-facing wall is perfect—with free-draining, rich soil.

PLANT PROFILE

HEIGHT 30ft (10m)

SITE Full sun or partial shade

SOIL Fertile, free-draining

HARDINESS Z9–10 H10–9

FLOWERING Spring

Stephanandra incisa 'Crispa'

IF HIGHLY EFFECTIVE GROUNDCOVER is what you're looking for, then try this low-growing shrub, which develops a dense, very wide-spreading thicket of deciduous stems. Interest extends year-round: greenish white flowers open in early summer (*see inset*), and before falling in autumn the leaves turn a vibrant reddish orange. Over winter the stems are an attractive, rich brown color. The parent plant, *Stephanandra incisa*, is larger and makes a graceful 6ft- (2m-) high tree with a spread of 10ft (3m). Both plants require moist but free-draining soil and full sun or light shade.

OTHER VARIETY *S. tanakae* (taller-growing, yellow-green flowers, orange-brown shoots, mid-green leaves turning orange and yellow).

PLANT PROFILE	
HEIGHT 24in (60cm)	
SPREAD 10ft (3m)	
SITE Full sun or partial shade	
SOIL Moist but free-draining	
HARDINESS Z3–8 H8–4	
FLOWERING Early summer	

Symphoricarpos albus var. *laevigatus* Snowberry

NO GUESSES HOW THE SNOWBERRY GOT ITS NAME. From autumn through to winter, the arching stems of this deciduous shrub are weighted down with round, white berries. These are preceded in summer by pink, bell-shaped flowers that are a magnet for bees. The snowberry is a thicket-forming shrub that grows just about anywhere, tolerating exposed sites and poor soil. Use it in wild or woodland gardens or as a screening hedge. Neaten up plants every few years by thinning out congested stems in early spring.

OTHER VARIETIES *S. x chenaultii* 'Hancock' (low and spreading, white flowers, dark pink berries); *S. x doorenbosii* (pink-blushed white berries); *S. orbiculatus* 'Foliis Variegatis' (yellow-margined leaves).

PLANT PROFILE
HEIGHT 6ft (2m)
SPREAD 6ft (2m)
SITE Full sun or partial shade
SOIL Preferably fertile, free-draining
HARDINESS Z3–7 H7–1
FLOWERING Summer

Symplocos paniculata Sapphire berry

THE TWIGGY, DECIDUOUS SAPPHIRE BERRY grows into a large shrub or small tree that is suitable for sunny, sheltered gardens. At the end of spring it puts on an amazing show, with branches densely packed with delicately scented, small, star-shaped white flowers (*see inset*). You will only get to see the metallic blue berries following a long, hot summer—another nearby plant for an exchange of pollen is essential, too. Slightly acidic soil is preferable, and it should also be rich and moist but free-draining.

PLANT PROFILE
HEIGHT 15ft (5m)
SPREAD 15ft (5m)
SITE Full sun
SOIL Acidic, fertile, moist but free-draining
HARDINESS Z5–8 H8–4
FLOWERING Late spring and early summer

Syringa vulgaris 'Charles Joly' Common lilac

MANY EXCELLENT, RICHLY SCENTED, deciduous lilacs are readily available, which can make it difficult to select the right one. 'Charles Joly', with its sweetly scented, dark purple flowers, is one of the best spreading types. Grow it as a hedge, at the back of a border, or as an individual specimen shrub. Best results will be achieved on rich, moist but free-draining soil. Deadhead the flower sprays as soon as they fade—otherwise, they will ruin the look of the shrub—and then prune the shrub after flowering.

OTHER VARIETIES *S. vulgaris* 'Firmament' (light blue flowers); *S. vulgaris* 'Madame Lemoine' (double white flowers); *S. vulgaris* 'Mrs Edward Harding' (double purple-red flowers).

PLANT PROFILE

HEIGHT 23ft (7m)

SPREAD 23ft (7m)

SITE Full sun

SOIL Fertile, moist but free-draining

HARDINESS Z4–8 H8–1

FLOWERING Late spring and early summer

Tamarix tetrandra Tamarisk

T

WITH MASSES OF THIN, SPINDLY STEMS almost completely covered in light pink flowers, this splendid shrub makes an arresting sight. It will struggle on anything other than very free-draining, preferably sandy soil—a coastal garden would suit it perfectly. After planting, cut the young plant back by half and then, in subsequent years, give it an annual pruning after flowering, cutting stems back to strong buds. As well as encouraging bushiness and maximum flowering, this treatment will stop it from getting top-heavy and falling over.

OTHER VARIETIES *T. parviflora* (larger-growing, purple shoots); *T. ramosissima* (larger-growing, red-brown shoots); *T. ramosissima* 'Pink Cascade' (rich pink flowers).

PLANT PROFILE
HEIGHT 10ft (3m)
SPREAD 10ft (3m)
SITE Full sun
SOIL Free-draining, sandy
HARDINESS Z5–9 H9–5
FLOWERING Mid- and late spring

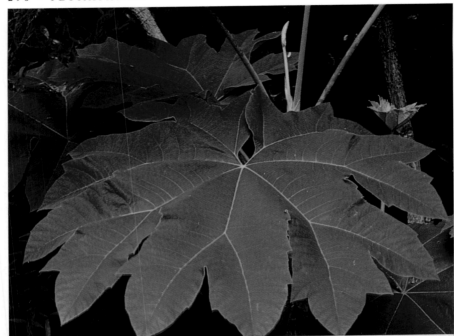

T

Tetrapanax papyrifer Rice-paper plant

WITH ITS SHAPELY LEAVES, up to 20in (50cm) long, the rice-paper plant makes a striking, architectural statement in the garden. When young, the scaly leaves carry a powdery covering; this quickly fades from the top surface, although it lingers on the underside of the leaf. White flowers appear in long, woolly panicles in autumn and attract bees. These are followed by small, round, black berries. If left unpruned, this suckering, thicket-forming evergreen will become leggy, but by cutting it hard back in early spring, to just 6in (15cm) above ground level, you will force up new, vigorous growth. Choose a sunny position sheltered from strong winds.

PLANT PROFILE	
HEIGHT 15ft (5m)	
SPREAD 15ft (5m)	
SITE Full sun	
SOIL Free-draining	
HARDINESS Z6–11 H12–6	
FLOWERING Autumn	

Teucrium fruticans Shrubby germander

T

SHORT AND BUSHY, this Mediterranean evergreen is worth growing for two reasons. First, it has aromatic, gray-green, silvery foliage, and second, it produces beautiful whorls of pale blue flowers (*see inset*). Its coloring makes it a good choice for pastel planting plans in which subtlety is called for. Some people find shrubby germander a rather untidy plant, but a light clip for shape in spring will keep it in check. Plant it in free-draining soil; avoid heavy clay at all costs.

OTHER VARIETIES *T. polium* (smaller, purple or yellow flowers, white-woolly, gray-green leaves); *T. subspinosum* (smaller, pink flowers, spiny).

PLANT PROFILE
HEIGHT 24–40in (60–100cm)
SPREAD 12ft (4m)
SITE Full sun
SOIL Free-draining
HARDINESS Z8–9 H9–8
FLOWERING Summer

T

Thymus 'Doone Valley' Thyme

THE DARK GREEN LEAVES OF THIS EVERGREEN thyme are distinctly marked with vibrant yellow spots, but it has only the faintest scent of lemon. Rather than planting it in the herb garden, use it in a rock garden or to fill gaps in a terrace, where it will thrive in the free-draining, poor soil and the reflected heat from the paving. A gentle trim after flowering is all that is needed to keep it shapely and to encourage bushiness.

OTHER VARIETIES *T.* x *citriodorus* 'Golden King' (taller-growing, gold-margined leaves); *T. herba-barona* (smaller-growing, pink flowers); *T. vulgaris* (taller-growing, purple to white flowers, aromatic leaves).

PLANT PROFILE
HEIGHT 5in (12cm)
SPREAD 14in (35cm)
SITE Full sun
SOIL Poor, free-draining
HARDINESS Z6–9
FLOWERING Summer

Trachelospermum jasminoides Star jasmine

T

TWISTING, TWINING, AND DELICATELY SCENTED, this evergreen climber will happily grow through support plants, such as holly, or it can be tied to wires and grown up a sunny, sheltered wall, or trained over a pergola. It goes particularly well with red and yellow roses or clematis. From midsummer it produces white flowers, while in winter its large, glossy green leaves turn reddish bronze. Given full sun and good drainage (so that the soil is never waterlogged), it makes an exotic plant for a sheltered garden. Prune lightly immediately after flowering, or in spring if it is outgrowing its allotted space.

OTHER VARIETY *T. asiaticum* (shorter-growing, fragrant creamy white flowers aging to yellow).

PLANT PROFILE

HEIGHT 28ft (9m)

SITE Full sun or partial shade

SOIL Free-draining, fertile

HARDINESS Z8–13 H12–6

FLOWERING Mid- and late summer

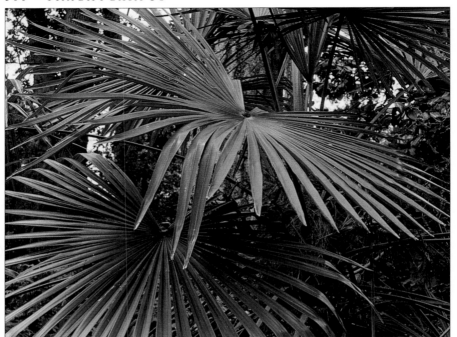

T

Trachycarpus fortunei Chusan palm

IN TIME, THE CHUSAN PALM WILL BECOME A GIANT—a tall, slender trunk topped with a crown of leaves. It is, however, slow-growing and initially quite shrubby. The fan-shaped leaves are the main focus, reaching up to 30in (75cm) long, and make a particularly attractive feature next to the vertical, straplike leaves of *Phormium tenax* (New Zealand flax). In its first few years this palm needs protection from freezing temperatures—packing straw around the crown provides good insulation—and shelter from the damaging effects of cold winds. Long, pendent spikes of yellow flowers appear in early summer, followed, on female plants, by blue-black fruit.

PLANT PROFILE	
HEIGHT 70ft (20m)	
SPREAD 8ft (2.5m)	
SITE Full sun or light shade	
SOIL Fertile, free-draining	
HARDINESS Z8–11 H12–8	
FLOWERING Early summer	

Tropaeolum speciosum Flame creeper

T

THERE SHOULD BE ROOM in most gardens for at least one of these climbers from South America. It sends up a mass of slender stems in early summer, bearing rich red flowers that look particularly good when trained through other climbers or dark green hedges, and over adjacent shrubs. Provide neutral to acidic, moist, rich soil, and a position where the roots are in the shade and the flowers in the sun. When the plant dies back in autumn, remove all the topgrowth and cover it with a protective mulch of compost.

OTHER VARIETIES *T. majus* 'Hermine Grashoff' (double, bright red flowers); *T. tuberosum* (orange and yellow flowers, veined with brown); *T. tuberosum* var. *lineamaculatum* 'Ken Aslet' (orange flowers).

PLANT PROFILE
HEIGHT 10ft (3m)
SITE Full sun or partial shade
SOIL Moist, fertile
HARDINESS Z8–11 H12–8
FLOWERING Summer to autumn

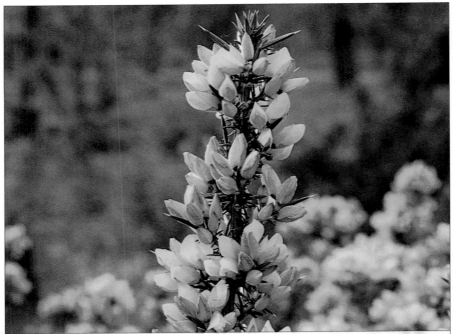

U

Ulex europaeus Gorse

FLASHY AND YELLOW-FLOWERED, this evergreen shrub is suitable for poor, acidic to neutral soils. The main show of color comes in the second half of spring, but it will then continue to flower intermittently throughout the year. Gorse is a densely twiggy, spine-packed shrub with dark brown seed pods that appear in summer—on hot sunny days they open with a loud crack. Grow it in a wild garden or on a dry, sunny slope. Every two or three years, after flowering, give it an all-over prune to keep it in shape.

OTHER VARIETIES *U. europaeus* 'Flore Pleno' (slightly more compact, double flowers); *U. gallii* (smaller-growing, pealike, bright yellow flowers, spine-tipped green shoots).

PLANT PROFILE

HEIGHT To 8ft (2.5m)

SPREAD 6ft (2m)

SITE Full sun

SOIL Poor, free-draining

HARDINESS Z6–8 H8–6

FLOWERING Second half of spring and later

Vaccinium glaucoalbum

V

THIS SUCKERING EVERGREEN SHRUB makes a dense thicket of stiff, broad, dark green leaves with white undersides. The pale pink flowers open at the end of spring and are followed by tiny, blue-black, white-bloomed, edible berries that last into winter. It is a strikingly attractive shrub with just one drawback—it needs a sunny, sheltered site and will not survive in cold climates. The soil should be acidic, peaty or sandy, and free-draining but moist. A light trim after it has flowered will keep it in good shape.

OTHER VARIETIES *V. corymbosum* (larger-growing, white flowers, edible blue-black berries); *V. nummularia* (smaller-growing, red-tipped pink flowers); *V. ovatum* (larger-growing, pink-flushed white flowers).

PLANT PROFILE

HEIGHT 20–48in (50–120cm)

SPREAD 3ft (1m)

SITE Full sun or partial shade

SOIL Acidic, moist but free-draining

HARDINESS Z9–11 H12–10

FLOWERING Late spring and early summer

THINNING OUT STEMS

Young plants should not be pruned at all. With established plants, remove up to one in five stems back to ground level to prevent congestion.

V *Viburnum* x *bodnantense* 'Dawn'

WITH ITS STRONG SCENT wafting around on still days, this plant is a must for the winter garden. The upward-pointing woody stems are bare at this time of year, save for small clusters of tiny pink flowers that age to white. These appear over a long period from late autumn to spring. *Viburnum* x *burkwoodii,* which flowers in spring, has the bonus of dark green, glossy, semievergreen leaves. Both thrive in average, free-draining soil, and can be pruned lightly after flowering.

OTHER VARIETIES   *V.* x *bodnantense* 'Charles Lamont' (bright pink flowers); *V.* x *burkwoodii* 'Anne Russell' (white fragrant flowers, compact); *V.* x *burkwoodii* 'Park Farm Hybrid' (dark pink flowers aging to white, leaves turn orange and red in autumn).

PLANT PROFILE
HEIGHT 10ft (3m)
SPREAD 6ft (2m)
SITE Full sun or partial shade
SOIL Average, free-draining
HARDINESS Z7–8 H8–7
FLOWERING Late autumn to spring

Viburnum opulus 'Compactum' Guelder rose

V

THE DECIDUOUS PARENT PLANT, *Viburnum opulus,* and its many cultivars grow vigorously and make huge bushes, but 'Compactum' is different, being slow-growing and, as its name suggests, quite compact. In early summer it produces flat sprays of white flowers followed, in autumn, by bright red berries (*see inset*). At this time of year the leaves also turn red before falling. In damp winter weather the plant may give off an unpleasant smell, but that's a small price to pay for such beauty. Prune out older stems after flowering to allow new growth to regenerate the bush.

OTHER VARIETY *V. opulus* 'Roseum' (white flowers, sometimes green-tinted, purple-tinted leaves in autumn).

PLANT PROFILE
HEIGHT 5ft (1.5m)
SPREAD 5ft (1.5m)
SITE Full sun or partial shade
SOIL Fertile, moist but free-draining
HARDINESS Z4–8 H8–1
FLOWERING Late spring and early summer

V *Viburnum plicatum* 'Mariesii' Wedding cake tree

THINK OF A DECIDUOUS BUSH WITH TIERED, horizontal branches covered in white flowers (*see inset*), and this plant's common name starts to make sense. The flowers are highlighted by dark green leaves that, by autumn, turn attractive shades of pink and purple. Such a vigorous shrub needs to go in a large border or a wild or woodland garden. 'Mariesii' thrives in most soils, provided they are well drained and fairly fertile. In gardens with heavy clay, grow it at the top of a slope where the drainage is better.

OTHER VARIETIES   *V. plicatum* 'Grandiflorum' (large heads of white flowers); *V. plicatum* 'Pink Beauty' (white flowers aging to pink); *V. plicatum* 'Rowallene' (compact, red-purple autumn leaves, red fruit).

PLANT PROFILE	
HEIGHT 10ft (3m)	
SPREAD 12ft (4m)	
SITE Sun or partial shade	
SOIL Fertile, free-draining	
HARDINESS Z4–8 H8–1	
FLOWERING Late spring	

Viburnums tend to produce new growth low on the main stem. To train them as standards, rub out new shoots on the trunk as they appear.

V

Viburnum tinus Laurustinus

EASILY GROWN AND RELIABLE, this evergreen provides a compact bush of dark green leaves and reddish twigs. The main attraction begins in late autumn when the flower buds start to fatten, and in mild spells they open to give a fine show of blooms from midwinter (later in colder areas) that continues well into spring. Blue-black fruit follows. This shrub does best in moist but free-draining soil.

OTHER VARIETIES *V. tinus* 'Gwenllian' (pink-tinged white flowers); *V. tinus* 'Pink Prelude' (white flowers aging to pink from pink buds); *V. tinus* 'Purpureum' (young bronze foliage); *V. tinus* 'Variegatum' (leaves margined with creamy yellow).

PLANT PROFILE

HEIGHT 10ft (3m)

SPREAD 10ft (3m)

SITE Full sun or partial shade

SOIL Moist but free-draining

HARDINESS Z8–10 H10–8

FLOWERING Late winter to spring

V | *Vitis coignetiae* Crimson glory vine

ONE OF THE MOST SPECTACULAR AUTUMN DISPLAYS of any climber is provided by this plant when its large, lobed leaves turn shades of red, yellow, and orange before falling. Make sure you have enough room for its prodigious growth, and ensure that the stems don't encroach onto a roof and dislodge shingles. Sturdy trees and large pergolas make good alternative climbing frames; excess growth can be removed in midwinter and midsummer. Given plenty of warmth and sun, tiny green flowers are followed by small, black (inedible) grapes. Provide a free-draining, rich soil.

OTHER VARIETY *V.* 'Brant' (bronze-red autumn leaves, edible blue-black grapes).

PLANT PROFILE

HEIGHT 50ft (15m)

SITE Full sun

SOIL Fertile, free-draining

HARDINESS Z5–9 H9–5

FLOWERING Summer

Weigela 'Looymansii Aurea'

PERK UP LATE-SPRING GARDENS with this slow-growing, rounded, deciduous shrub that combines an abundant show of bell-shaped pink flowers with arching stems of golden yellow leaves. Pruning involves cutting flowered shoots back to a vigorous bud as soon as the flowers fade. When the plant is mature, cut about a fourth of the old stems back to the base annually. For best results, plant it in free-draining, rich soil.

OTHER VARIETIES *W.* 'Abel Carrière' (larger-growing, dark pink-red flowers with yellow-spotted throats); *W.* 'Bristol Ruby' (larger-growing, dark red flowers); *W.* 'Praecox Variegata' (creamy yellow-margined leaves).

PLANT PROFILE	
HEIGHT 5ft (1.5m)	
SPREAD 5ft (1.5m)	
SITE Partial shade	
SOIL Fertile, free-draining	
HARDINESS Z5–9	
FLOWERING Late spring and early summer	

W · *Wisteria floribunda* 'Multijuga'

THERE ARE TWO WELL-KNOWN TYPES OF WISTERIA: Chinese (*Wisteria sinensis*) and Japanese (*W. floribunda*). Chinese types are more popular because they generally climb higher and have larger flowers with a stronger scent. However, they flower in late spring, when their whole crop of blooms can be caught by frost. 'Multijuga' is useful because the flowers of this Japanese type open later, at the start of summer, when its long, pendent flowering stems can reach up to 4ft (1.2m). Grow it in free-draining, well-watered soil against a wall or up a sturdy tree.

OTHER VARIETIES *W. floribunda* 'Alba' (white flowers); *W. floribunda* 'Rosea' (pink flowers).

PLANT PROFILE
HEIGHT 28ft (9m) or more
SITE Full sun or partial shade
SOIL Moist but free-draining
HARDINESS Z5–9 H9–5
FLOWERING Early summer

Xanthoceras sorbifolium Yellowhorn

WHY THIS DELIGHTFUL, DECIDUOUS CHINESE SHRUB isn't a more common sight in gardens is a mystery. Its native habitat of scrubby areas and woodland edge makes it an easy plant to grow. It will thrive in a large border or woodland garden if given fertile, free-draining soil and plenty of sun. The star-shaped, lightly scented white flowers coincide with the appearance of its new leaves. The flowers have contrasting dark red centers, and the leaves start off pale green but gradually become darker as they mature. This shrub should be pruned after flowering.

PLANT PROFILE

HEIGHT 12ft (4m)

SPREAD 10ft (3m)

SITE Full sun

SOIL Fertile, free-draining

HARDINESS Z5–8 H8–5

FLOWERING Late spring

Y *Yucca filamentosa* 'Bright Edge' Adam's needle

STRIPED GREEN AND YELLOW, the swordlike leaves erupt out of the ground, making 'Bright Edge' a top-quality architectural plant. Just watch out for the needlelike spines on the leaf tips. In summer it sends up sturdy 6ft (2m) spikes packed with lightly scented, white flowers. Since excellent drainage is a necessity, it grows best in free-draining soil in a Mediterranean-style garden or on a sunny slope. It will also appreciate the sharp drainage in a large pot. Create a mixed yucca display with the frost-hardy *Yucca whipplei* and *Y. gloriosa*.

OTHER VARIETIES *Y. filamentosa* 'Variegata' (white-margined, blue-green leaves); *Y. flaccida* 'Golden Sword' (yellow-margined leaves); *Y. flaccida* 'Ivory' (creamy white flowers).

PLANT PROFILE	
HEIGHT 30in (75cm)	
SPREAD 5ft (1.5m)	
SITE Full sun	
SOIL Free-draining	
HARDINESS Zx–x Hx–x	
FLOWERING Mid- and late summer	

Yushania anceps 'Pitt White' Fountain bamboo

Y

THIS HIGHLY INVASIVE, EVERGREEN BAMBOO from India has glossy deep green canes that initially shoot bolt upright. In time, however, they arch over under the weight of the leaves, which can grow to 5⅓in (14cm) long. Don't even think about growing a plant as vigorous as this in a small garden, but where space allows, exploit its rampant tendencies and use it as a perimeter hedge or screen, or as a specimen plant for a wild garden where you can work around the plant to dig out any excess growth. Ideally, this bamboo needs rich, moist but free-draining soil, and a sheltered spot out of cold winter winds, which may damage the leaves.

PLANT PROFILE

HEIGHT 12ft (4m)

SPREAD Indefinite

SITE Full sun or partial shade

SOIL Moist, fertile, free-draining

HARDINESS Z7–10

Z *Zanthoxylum piperitum* Japan pepper

ALTHOUGH THE FLOWERS ARE INSIGNIFICANT, this deciduous, spiny bush has very attractive foliage with 6in- (15cm-) long, glossy, dark green leaves that turn yellow in autumn. Tear up a leaf and it will immediately release a strong, aromatic scent. The small, early-summer flowers are followed by tiny red berries that split open to reveal black seeds. Bite into one and you will instantly detect a peppery heat; they are, in fact, used as a pepper substitute in Japan. It will grow in most gardens but must have free-draining, fertile soil.

OTHER VARIETY *Z. simulans* (larger-growing, warty red fruit, large, glossy dark green leaves turning reddish-yellow in autumn).

PLANT PROFILE
HEIGHT 8ft (2.5m)
SPREAD 8ft (2.5m)
SITE Full sun or light shade
SOIL Fertile, free-draining
HARDINESS Z6–9 H9–6
FLOWERING Early summer

Zenobia pulverulenta Honeycup

Z

AN UNDERRATED SHRUB, zenobia mixes well with rhododendrons, enjoying the same acidic, moist, rich soil. Over the course of the year it is quite colorful, with young leaves that carry a blue tinge before turning deep, glossy green, followed by clusters of dainty, bell-shaped, scented white flowers that appear in early summer. In autumn, it puts on a magnificent display when its leaves redden before falling. There are two pruning regimens to follow: give it a medium trim after flowering has finished, cutting back to vigorous buds; then, every four years, be more severe, cutting it back close to the base to force up strong, new, vigorous growth.

PLANT PROFILE

HEIGHT 6ft (2m)

SPREAD 5ft (1.5m)

SITE Sun or partial shade

SOIL Acidic, moist, fertile

HARDINESS Z5–8 H8–5

FLOWERING Early and midsummer